Unmoored

How I Got Swept Away by Two Affairs – and Managed to Save My Marriage

Monika Patton

Unmoored: How I Got Swept Away by Two Affairs – and Managed to Save My Marriage

Copyright 2019 by Monika Patton

The information given in this book should not be treated as a substitute for professional medical advice; always consult a medical practitioner. Any use of information in this book is at the reader's discretion and risk. The author cannot be held responsible for any loss, claim or damage arising out of the use, or misuse, of the suggestions made, the failure to take medical advice for any material on third-party websites.

ISBN: 978-1-79645-629-5

TABLE OF CONTENTS

Introduction

I just wanted to tell you what a great day today was. I loved being online with you...God you're so beautiful, so incredibly sexy and I feel like we're really starting to connect very deeply with each other. I feel like we're becoming even better friends, and that makes me really, really happy.

I love feeling closer to you each night before I go to bed, and tonight I feel so very, very close to you ... even more a part of you than I did this morning. I really cannot express the love I have for you, but more importantly the really profound NEED I have to be with you, to have you a part of me ... my life ... my every day. I can't imagine a life without you in it ... just the thought of it crushes me utterly. I'm so thankful that we are we ... that we somehow, someway found each other... I will never let you go, you are my life, my future ... my love.

I never set out to have an affair, let alone two affairs. I never entertained the idea of hurting my husband, my kids, me – or our parents, siblings, family or friends. I didn't think about breaking

1

apart and ripping down and stomping to pieces the life we – I – had built.

But it happened anyway.

A marriage that looked perfectly fine from the outside was slowly rotting away, little by little. It was hard to see the rot, even for us, the two people who were in the marriage. Marriages are like that. They are complex structures with so many hidden nooks and crannies. It can be hard to see those parts – unless you are paying attention. Or bothering to look.

Marriages can appear strong on the outside, but tear away that bright shininess, and what do you find? Fragile bits that have been haphazardly duct taped together on the inside. That was my marriage. It was duct taped.

Duct tape is strong, but it's not a permanent fix. Eventually, it comes undone, and then you have a real mess on your hands. Instead of spending the time and money (aka, going to marriage counseling) to make the proper repairs, we ignored the problems. And then it all came crashing down.

In just eight months, I completely destroyed my life. During the next three months, I could barely function. Then I slowly started to rebuild, a wrenching experience that involved convincing my husband, who I'll call E. in this book, to take me back.

And guess what?

My 13-month journey through hell was worth it. It opened my eyes to who I really was, who E. was and the changes we both needed to make in our relationship. In fact, having two affairs, leaving E. and ruining our lives *saved our marriage*.

You read that right. Behaving like an out-of-control teenager and destroying my marriage actually saved it. That's pretty messed up.

It also saved me. When the first affair started, I had completely lost myself. I didn't know who I was anymore. If you don't know who you are, you cannot behave rationally. As Captain Obvious might helpfully point out, having two affairs back-to-back is not healthy behavior. As the second affair began and rapidly progressed, I became a different person, a person who I definitely did not like. It got to the point that I didn't even recognize the person staring back at me in the mirror. Affairs muddy the waters; they do not provide any clarity at all.

Once my life collapsed, I had to work really, really hard to fix myself. I had to make peace with my actions and increase my self-awareness. This was on top of working, taking care of my kids, grocery shopping, doing laundry and just trying to get through each day. It was so fucking hard. But I didn't care. I just kept marching forward. I wanted to be more patient, kinder, more generous, more thoughtful and more loving. I wanted to be less judgmental, less angry and less anxious. And now I am. Also, I'm on Zoloft. Don't discount the effects of a good prescription drug.

So why am I sharing this very intimate, gut-wrenching story?

Because of the rare – some would say miraculous – ending. The trauma caused by two – not one but two! – affairs didn't end our marriage. It left us bruised and battered, but those are injuries that heal over time. Once E. and I both healed, we were able to build a better and stronger marriage – much happier and much stronger than it ever was or ever could have been. If our marriage had once been as flimsy as the first little pig's straw house, it is now the third little pig's rock-solid brick house (complete with fireplace to destroy the bad guys).

I am also sharing because I want to help people who are in the same position as I once was. Affairs are very isolating. You might not be able to tell anyone. So now you are stuck carrying around this huge, very heavy secret that grows bigger by the day. That's exhausting. You will likely spend more time by yourself.

But affairs aren't just physically isolating, they are socially and emotionally isolating. Let's say you choose to unload some of the secret on your best friend. You cross your fingers that BF reacts well. When they do, it's such a relief. Finally, someone you can talk to! But they can only be supportive to a certain extent. Unless they have also gone through an affair, they can't quite empathize with you. And they might not want to. They might be upset with you and end up backing away.

I lost a lot of friends. Some quietly withdrew from my life because they didn't know what to do. Others completely turned their backs on me. There was a lot of gossip. A lot of finger pointing. And a lot of heartache. Of my large circle of friends, only five stood by me throughout the affairs. Two very close friends who were like an aunt and uncle to our kids completely vilified me. When E. and I got back together, that friendship was permanently destroyed.

Let's talk about why affairs happen for a minute, because this is very important to understand. Men have affairs for one reason that's pretty much common knowledge: Not enough sex in the marriage. Women have affairs because they're not getting the attention and recognition they need in their marriage. Sex is secondary or even tertiary for women.

That quote at the top of this introduction? That was written by the second guy, the one who let me – even encouraged me – to destroy my marriage. Seductive, isn't it?

But that kind of intense attention from a source that is not your spouse is not kosher. Not enough sex and not enough attention are big problems. Any problems in a marriage tend to get compounded by children, careers, late-night runs to CVS for cough medicine, and arguing over whose turn it is to take out the garbage. In my marriage, these problems crowded out love, contentment and joy and opened the door to resentment, sarcasm and anger.

Love notes sent via email in the middle of the night from a stranger are not a solution to anything. Instead, I had to create my own solution.

If you're contemplating an affair, having an affair or trying to get out of an affair, please know that you are not alone. Far from it. No matter how smart and accomplished you are, you are vulnerable. In my case, I was vulnerable to a cruel and manipulative person who was all too ready to pounce when he finally got the chance. That's a dangerous place to find oneself. If you're foundering in your life or marriage – or if you're already lost – an affair will not help fix the situation. The grass is not greener on the other side. Intellectually, you know that, but I had to say it anyway.

Marriage is really, really hard but separation and divorce proceedings are harder, more draining and more expensive. We are still paying down debt we accumulated during our separation (E. hired the best attorney he couldn't afford). Before you try to exit the marriage, get thee to therapy. A good therapist is cheaper than a good divorce attorney.

OK, enough lecturing.

This is my story.

Chapter 1

The Beginning

It was April 2011, and E., our two kids, and I were flying east, speeding along at 35,000 feet on a plane bound for Amsterdam. So, you know, it was a typical spring break ... but with passports.

For three days, we toted our 4-year old son and 8-year old daughter all over the city. E. was born and grew up in a small suburb outside of Amsterdam, so it was like being home. The food was familiar, the language was familiar, the bicycles everywhere were familiar. But the weather was not familiar.

Instead of overcast skies and gloomy rain, the Netherlands was experiencing postcard-perfect weather. Every day was warm and sunny. The locals flocked to parks and outdoor cafes, and we followed suit. Then we discovered that cafes – serving alcohol! – were conveniently located adjacent to every single park we walked by. The parks all had big playgrounds. We were in heaven. "Now this – this is what we need in the US," E. and I kept saying. Instead of the kids dragging us to playgrounds, we were dragging them to playgrounds – after a quick stop at the café for a Heineken.

After exploring Amsterdam and its parks, we de-camped to the countryside, where my husband's family lives. Our home away from home was a circa-1680 farmhouse-turned-B&B 2 km from his aunt and uncle's horse farm. It came complete with a thatched roof, impossibly white goose-down comforters and breakfast spreads that crowded the dining room table. Days were spent touring centuries-old towns and visiting the homes and neighborhoods where grandparents, aunts and uncles grew up. Evenings were spent relaxing on the patio with family. It was truly an idyllic vacation.

We returned home happy and ready to settle back into real life. Our routines of school, soccer, swim classes, piano lessons, errands, neighborhood gatherings and work began again.

This is when my life began to shift. The shift happened so slowly that it was imperceptible – almost invisible. Just like you can't see your child grow in the moment, I was not aware that my life was changing. The shift came in the form of work - a new colleague, who, like me, worked as a contractor for a media company.

At this point, my company was two years old. I was still running around to networking events, buzzing in and out of conversations, meeting new people, forming new business relationships. Business was finally taking off, and we were thrilled. E. had been my champion, beaming with pride every time I announced a new client or project.

Well, with all this work came a lot of attention. Attention from people outside the marriage. I ignored it at first. The occasional crass remark and the leering gaze left me shaking my head. I'd retreat to my sweet little family, relieved that I could unwind and snuggle on the couch with the people who loved me the most.

***

I fell in love at first sight with E. on March 14, 1997. I was a 22-year old senior at university in New York, itching to graduate and conquer the world. I had it all planned. First, I would move to San Diego. I had never been to San Diego, but family friends lived there and loved it. The lifestyle and weather – perfection. So much better than the fast-paced lifestyle I grew up with on the East Coast.

Second, I would land a fabulous job in marketing and conquer the business world. I'd work in an office with other young, smart people. I'd collaborate on fun, impactful projects and share brilliant ideas in team meetings. I'd make a lot of friends, build an active social life, life in a cute bungalow by the water and, most importantly, go to the beach all. The. Time. Life would be grand!

Before I could answer the siren song of San Diego, I had final exams to pass – and a marketing conference to help plan. I was a marketing major and sat on the board of our school's American Marketing Association chapter. Our professor had thrown out the idea of organizing a business day for students. The idea was simple: Students could learn about various careers from a hodgepodge network of friends and alumnae. The students who attended would cobble together a firmer idea of what their career could look like. It would be swell.

On the day of the conference, I woke up to a surprise spring snowstorm. As the morning wore on and the snow didn't let up, our speakers slowly trickled in. By 10am, everyone had arrived except for one. Well, we shrugged our shoulders, he'll show up eventually.

The conference began. We were lined up at long rows of tables in a vast meeting room. The introductory remarks were complete, and the keynote speaker was about to begin.

Across from the room, a door swung open and I froze. In he walked, a huge smile plastered on his face. It hit me like a bolt of lightning. I leaned over to my friend Michelle and said, "That's E."

"How do you know?" she whispered back.

9

"I just do."

And like that, I was in love … at first sight.

I made it my business to strike up a conversation with him as soon as humanly possible. I escorted him to and from meeting rooms and I generally hovered near him. After the conference, speakers, professors and those of us who organized the day's events gathered at a cocktail reception off campus. I never left E.'s side, and he didn't mind one bit.

At this point, I'd known him for all of six hours but I felt like I'd known him forever. He's incredibly easy to talk to and comfortable in any situation. He has an easy laugh and a big smile. He constantly cracks jokes – and laughs at all of them, which makes me laugh even more. Being with him was like being rolled up into a warm hug. It was – and still is – an incredible feeling.

We talked and laughed and flirted for the next eight hours. At some point, it stopped snowing. When the reception was over, we moved to a bar in town. We finally left around 2am and made plans for a date the next evening. Then we kissed good night – and I practically floated home.

Our first date lasted 11 hours. He picked me up at 6pm on Saturday, and he dropped me off at 5am on Sunday. He called me on his drive back to Boston Sunday afternoon. At that moment, I knew he was mine and that we'd get married … and that I wasn't moving to San Diego.

We began talking on the phone every night, and he kept asking when I was coming to visit him in Boston. He worked full-time, I was in school full-time, and I worked weekends. I finally wrangled a weekend off and made the three-hour drive to Boston.

That weekend was a fuzzy blur of joy, contentment, sex and laughter. I met his friends from grad school. He showed me where he worked. We hung out with his roommate, and we did tourist stuff. But mostly, we had a lot of fun. I didn't want to leave his side. Ever.

Then at long last, I graduated. E. was there for graduation, of course, and he fit right in with my friends and family. I spent a few days with him in Boston before my friend Anna and I flew to Europe for a month of backpacking. Remember, this was 1997, so there was no WhatsApp or FaceTime. A month was a long time to be separated, especially since we didn't talk at all. Well, I did call him once from Bologna to announce that I was eating the best focaccia ever. It was 6am in Boston when I called. He and his roommate were not amused when the phone rang at that hour, but I was high on life and thrilled to hear his groggy voice. As Anna and I traveled around Italy and southern France, we made a lot of new friends from all over the world. We wandered around Florence with a woman from Australia – who we saw again in Cinque Terre. We met a young, recovering lawyer from Seattle at our hostel in Siena. We drove with him to Rome the next day and spent three days touring the ancient city before we headed in separate directions. In Cinque Terre, we found two roommates – one from Australia and one from San Francisco – who we shared an apartment with. We also met two guys who ended up traveling to Nice with us via train. We were instant friends and had a great time the few days we were together. But E. was always on my mind and in my conversations. It was very clear to every guy we met that I was besotted with someone back home.

I returned home to the states, ready for my life in Boston. Yes, Boston has the opposite attitude, weather and lifestyle of San Diego. It didn't matter. All that mattered was being with E. From the get-go, we were like a little old married couple - never mind that I was 22 and he was 27 when we met. Our relationship just felt so natural. In 1999, we moved in together and got engaged. In 2000, we married.

As easy as it was to build our life together and embark on marriage, I was struggling. I hated Boston. I couldn't make any friends, which was a new phenomenon to me. No one would ever describe me as a wallflower. I love people. I love meeting new people, I love talking to people, I love doing stuff with people. For a people-person, Boston was a shock of cold, angry water. It is a very insular city. If you didn't grow up or attend university there, it's hard to break into the friend groups that already exist. The attitude was, "We have all the friends we need, so no thanks!"

On top of being incredibly lonely in a town overflowing with people my age, work sucked. My first job out of college was assistant to an attorney at an institutional wealth management company. Sexy, no? Believe it or not, it was a fabulous company to work for. I happened to be working for the one dragon lady out of thousands of employees. She was so bad that she couldn't hold onto assistants. Most lasted around a year. I left after five months, completely disenchanted and disappointed with "real life".

Then I landed at a pre-dotcom tech startup. Boston was flooded with them at time. Our office was out in the suburbs, and my colleagues consisted of engineers who were married with kids. Snooze-fest.

I became increasingly reliant on E. for everything – love, attention, nurturing, and patience. And my gosh, he had patience – vast stores of it. No matter how anxious and frustrated I was, he provided nothing but love and support and encouragement. I found stress-relief and dragged joy into my life by going for long walks every day and cooking obsessively.

When I announced, "I think I want to launch a personal chef business," the response was, "Yes, honey that's great! You'll be fabulous at it!" And I was, but being a personal chef was not what I expected. You think people are weird? Wait til you start cooking for them. I'll have to write another book about them, so here's a snapshot of who I was working for: One guy faked a Russian accent for a few months, one family was "gluten free" but would happily eat couscous, and a couple wanted me to cancel my vacation plans so I could cook for their July 4 BBQ. I cannot make this shit up. I stuck it out until a month before our wedding. I was burned out and needed a job with a steadier income and slightly less-crazy people in my life. So, I became a nanny to the kids of a pro hockey player.

In May of 2001, we moved to Virginia. E. got a new job, and the pro hockey player and his family moved back home to Toronto. We found a charming brick house in Arlington to rent, so while I was turning it into a home, I applied for jobs. I landed one that was tolerable. I didn't love it, but I will readily admit that I hated Mondays. I never wanted to go to work, but I was an adult and I went anyway. Then a colleague stole my wallet, and that was it. I had had enough. I quit with E.'s full support.

Two weeks later, morning sickness kicked in. That spring, we bought a house, and in 2002, our daughter arrived. E. was over the moon. She was a wonderful, happy little baby. Given my track record in the career department thus far, we agreed that I should stay home with her. I made new friends – friends with babies – and though there were plenty of days I was bored out of my gourd, being a mom was fine for the time being. I didn't have to worry about dragon lady bosses, weird customers or thieves disguised as colleagues. Life was quiet, and we were happy. We went to the beach, we accompanied E. on work trips, we picnicked at wineries, we attended kids' birthday parties, we did yard work together, and we had fun. Life wasn't perfect, but it was our life.

In 2006, we welcomed our son to the family. A week after we brought him home from the hospital, I distinctly remember sitting up in bed, surrounded by pillows and nursing this tiny creature with curly blonde hair. Our 3-year old daughter was sleeping down the hall. E. quietly crept into our room to get ready for bed. And I was in this pure state of bliss and contentment. Life was just as it was meant to be.

I had a sweet little family. My kids were happy and healthy. My husband loved me.

But there were little fissures in our relationships, hair line cracks that were nearly invisible to the naked eye. They'd been there since the beginning, of course, but at this point – six years into our marriage and nine years into our relationship – they were starting to affect the foundation that was holding up our marriage.

Much – but certainly not all of it – was me. Quite by accident, I was raised with an unhealthy sense of entitlement, inflated self-worth and complete lack of resilience. Before I go further, I want to say that I had a wonderful childhood. My parents, two brothers and I don't just love each other, we genuinely like each other, and we remain close to this day. In fact, one of our favorite things to do is sit around and swap "remember that one time?" stories.

I do, however, understand why I was entitled and why I lacked resilience. My dad grew up in a war zone in Europe during and after WWII. His father abandoned him, his brother and mom. He almost died at age two. In short, his childhood was not filled with cupcakes and daisies. He did everything he could to give us the childhood he didn't have, and that included shielding us from hurt and criticism, praising us and making it clear that we deserved only the best. This is how I became entitled. But even worse? I was never corrected. If I behaved badly, excuses were made. Blame was laid on others, or my behavior was ignored.

I was also raised by a parent who was (and still is) judgmental and critical. I observed this behavior – and modeled it. If E. tried to help with the baby, I would tell him he was doing "it" wrong – whatever "it" was in that moment. If he made dinner, I'd hover over him, criticizing his knife skills or the way he was organizing the vegetables on the counter. Never mind that there are many perfectly good ways to pile vegetables on the counter.

I'd openly make fun of people when we were out and about, all while feeling very smug with how perfect I was. One summer afternoon, we were sitting on a bench in a public garden people-watching. I turned it into a running monologue of nonstop criticism. I called out people for being overweight, badly dressed, stupid-looking – you name it. E. finally had enough and told me to shut up. I clammed up immediately, but unfortunately, being corrected was a rarity. So, my behavior never changed.

I was also impatient. If E. wasn't doing something fast enough, I'd yell at him. If a driver was driving slowly in the passing line, I'd yell at ... my windshield. I'd complain loudly if the line at the store was moving too slowly. When the doctor was running behind, I'd harangue the poor receptionist.

I was quick to anger, and I was a yeller. I was an unpredictable yeller. You never knew when I'd get pissed off or what I'd get pissed about. And then I would explode. (I later learned that my mother-in-law was scared of me because I was so volatile. I am not proud of that.)

This constant barrage of criticism and yelling affected our marriage. E. began to think he couldn't do anything right. His self-esteem was slowly depleted. In an act of self-preservation, he began to withdraw. I was exhausting him, so he stopped fighting me and let me have my way. All the while, he remained as lovely and loving as can be. I ran rough shod over him, and he still smiled.

Wow. I sound like a total asshole! Rest assured, I did not behave like this every minute of every day. I'm actually a very happy, positive person. I'm smart, energetic, curious, funny and laugh a lot. But I do have a dark side – we all do – and you just learned all about mine. Was that easy to share? Yes and no. Yes, because I have taken full responsibility for who I was. No, because, hell, who in their right mind gets excited about flinging open their ugly, skeleton-filled closet?

But now you know who I was, which helps explains how I fell into two affairs.

***

Let's go back to spring 2011 when my business was taking off. After essentially being ignored as a stay-at-home mom for seven long years, I mattered. I mattered not to just my family and friends, but to strangers and clients and new people who were coming into my life. I was receiving praise and attention and smiles and laughter from new people, and I was gobbling it up. And I was making money! For the first time in a long time, I was earning a living and contributing to household expenses. I mattered.

I was so invigorated that I began to let work interfere. All that praise and attention morphed into an addiction. I began wanting more. The want turned into an overriding need for a steady supply. The steady supply was never enough. And that's when it dawned on me. I wasn't getting enough attention at home. How often did E. tell me I looked beautiful? Or that he loved a dress on me? Or that I was simply amazing? Close to never. I had no idea I was remotely attractive or that I was still an interesting human being until people – men – outside my marriage began telling me. No. Idea. My husband didn't tell me, so now other people were stepping into the void.

And that's when the first affair began. I had run into Will a few times at various events. One evening, a perfectly normal conversation turned into mild flirtation that turned into a 12-hour texting marathon the next day. The compliments flowed off the screen and enveloped me. I was hooked. Here was a very handsome, very successful guy interested in ME. Me!

We met up a week later and made out in his car in a parking garage. Soon after that we set up secret email accounts, and we began sneaking around in plain sight. We planned nooners and had sex in cars. It was a very short and very intense affair that consumed both of our lives. Interestingly, my brain used my body to rebel against what was happening. I lost my appetite and several pounds. I stopped sleeping. But I didn't care. This affair filled a gaping void in my life (and his). I was constantly hearing how beautiful, smart, funny and sexy I was, and he was getting tons of sex, which was almost nonexistent in his marriage.

I don't blame Will at all for this affair. We were equally complicit in it. Neither of us took advantage of the other person. We didn't lie to each other. We didn't hurt each other. We simply acted like selfish idiots and had a lot of fun in the process.

But as fun and exhilarating as it was, sneaking around took up a lot of time and energy. We started to get sloppy – we'd literally drive around parking garages to find a secluded spot. We'd call each other on weekends and evenings. The fun affair began to turn into a burden. By mid-summer, I told him that no good could come of it. We weren't going to leave our families, and continuing this affair wasn't going to help our marriages. We tearfully agreed to end it, right at the beginning of his annual summer vacation.

I clearly remember that conversation. Will and I were texting furiously. I was home alone as usual. The kids were at camp. E. was at work. I finally put down my Blackberry and stared out the window, feeling very lost.

Now what? I thought. I wasn't happy with E. – that much was obvious – but I had never once thought about leaving him, either. I didn't know what to do next.

The void was back. So I picked my Blackberry back up and called Ryan.

***

Before I begin the next part of our story, obviously, Ryan is not his name. It's a great name, but a blockhead of an ex-boyfriend ruined it for me decades ago. It seems a fitting name for the guy who let me trash my life.

Ryan had been waiting in the wings for months. When I called him, I flung open a door he had been trying to unlock since April. That when he joined the media company I was already working with. It was now early August. For four months, he had been steadily working to get my attention. Ever so slowly, he crept into my life. He was like a rising tide. At first, I didn't notice. Then I had to pick up my beach chair and move back a few yards, but the tide came higher. The next thing I knew, I was practically sitting in the water. I moved again. And again. But still the tide came. And suddenly it surrounded me.

Our relationship in April was completely professional. I was the Editor at the media company, and he was the graphic designer. We talked pretty much every day via Basecamp (a project management platform). Our exchanges were basic: "I need images for these three articles, please. Could you get them to me by 10am?" "Sure thing," he'd reply.

As we got to know each other – and as he began to notice me – the exchanges became chummier.

"Good morning! I need four images this morning for these four articles, but you only need to get me the first three by 10am. The fourth one is for an article that will publish tomorrow first thing. Thanks so much!"

"As you wish," became his standard response.

If you're a big fan of the 1987 movie (and cult classic) "The Princess Bride", you'll immediately recognize that phrase. "As you wish" was code for "I love you." I didn't pick up on it, because I hadn't seen the movie since, like, forever. I had no idea that Ryan was doing anything untoward. The tide was rising, but I didn't know it yet.

What I did know was that Ryan was a very good graphic designer who lived in Colorado and never missed a deadline.

In June, Ryan texted me a few times during the week. I always responded, because it was always about work. Then he texted me on a weekend. His wife and kids were visiting her family on the East Coast, so he was home alone. He sent me a photo of his dog – his dinner companion that night. Cute.

"Why on Earth is Ryan texting me about his dog?" I wondered. "I don't really know him. I don't really care that he's home alone on a Saturday. Yay, good for you. I don't care!"

I moved my beach chair back a few yards.

Random texts and emails began arriving. Not every day, but they often showed up on weekends. He was working, he missed our interactions, so he'd text me. I vividly remember receiving a text from him while I was at the pool with E., the kids and a bunch of our friends.

"What are you up to on this lovely Saturday afternoon?"

18

"I'm at the pool."

"I bet you're the most beautiful woman there."

"You're making me blush! I doubt it, but thanks."

"Oh no - I'm sure of it. All the guys are jealous that you're not with them."

"Ha – that's a good one. Are you working?"

"Yeah. I have a bunch of projects to catch up on."

"OK, have fun. Talk to you Monday."

"As you wish. Bye beautiful!"

That's sweet. And weird. But whatever. Remember, I was very busy running around with Will. I had no time to think about Ryan, let alone ponder his motives.

About a week later, I got a text.

"Hey – can you talk real quick?"

"Sure," I replied.

My phone rang. It was mid-afternoon.

"Hello? Ryan?"

"Hi Monika! Um, so I'm here in Chicago for the Media Company event…"

"Oh yeah, that was last night! How was it?"

"Good – really good. I was surprised you weren't there."

"Well, they didn't really invite me or offer to pay my way, so … yeah, I'm not there."

"Got it. Bummer."

He paused.

"I know this is kind of strange," he continued, "but I didn't know who else to call. I want to get a gift for my wife and daughter, and I'm in this mall in Chicago, and I have no idea what to buy them."

"Hmm. Well, I don't know them, but I have yet to meet a woman who doesn't love to receive jewelry as a gift. Could you get them earrings or a necklace? What about a ring? Not sure what they might like. How old is your daughter?"

"She's 15. Maybe I could get her a necklace. Not sure what my wife would like, but this is really helpful. I'm so glad I called you."

"Happy to help! Good luck. How much longer are you in Chicago?"

"I fly home tomorrow."

"OK, have a safe flight. Talk to you later!"

"OK thanks. Bye Monika!"

I hung up the phone. "That was really fucking weird," I said out loud. "I don't understand what just happened."

I looked down at my phone, still in my hand. Why did he call me? I don't know him. We just work together, for Pete's sake! Yet he keeps reaching out to me.

I shrugged my shoulders, turned my attention back to my computer screen and went back to work.

The tide was lapping at my feet.

Three weeks later, it all clicked into place.

Chapter 2

A House of Cards

So here's when I knew I was in love with you ... was thinking about this in bed this morning. When I was in Chicago, I went up to the lake around sunset on Friday night. It was still stiflingly hot and humid, but I found a nice (semi) cool spot and just was sitting and felt very chill.

And I was thinking that there was only one person that I wanted next to me at that moment ... and it was you - a woman I hardly knew. I laughed out loud, it was so ridiculous. But I knew ... I felt it down deep ... that there was some reason I was thinking this completely retarded thought ... so then I knew ... I knew it would happen, but didn't know how or when or any of that ... but I just knew.

Because when I was stopped dead in my tracks by your video up on the screen in the bar the night before ... TRYING to get everyone to shut the fuck up ... I knew.

Now you know why he called me from Chicago. Ryan attended the media company's 10-year anniversary party because he thought at long last he'd meet me in person. Instead, he saw my video message, part of a montage created for the company founder. I later learned that he reserved two hotel rooms for that trip. One in a very posh hotel, and one in a regular hotel. If I attended, he was going to somehow sweep me off my feet and ferry me off to the posh hotel.

***

Three weeks after Ryan called me from Chicago, I ended the affair with Will. That's when I called Ryan. I was upset and confused and just needed to talk this out with someone. Only one friend knew about the affair, and she was drowning in her own disastrous marriage.

Because he had been like a rising tide since April, Ryan suddenly became the best person to call. He only vaguely knew me, but he seemed to make himself available. That's what I needed: a fairly objective person to talk to. Little did I know that he was not at all objective. His original goal was to get on my radar. His new goal was to meet me. And his pipe-dream goal was to have an affair. Of course, hindsight is a very sharp 20/20, but on that day in August, my brain was muddled. I was completely overwhelmed. The tide had overtaken my beach chair.

We talked for two hours.

I spilled my guts. Everything that I had been holding in – about my marriage, the affair, the sneaking around, the emotional exhaustion – rushed out in a torrent. Ryan was a very sympathetic listener, and he was all too eager to praise me, soothe me, hold my hand and become a shoulder to cry on.

It was huge relief for me. I was finally able to shed the clutter and clean out the muck. The light was shining on the darkest part of my life, making it less scary and more hopeful. Everything felt like it would be OK. Somehow, my life would be OK.

We ended the call because Ryan had to pick up his kids from school. "Call me tomorrow if you need to talk," he said.

The next day, we talked for three hours.

Ryan made it clear he was available to me, so he became my lifeline. We started talking every day, and we didn't stop talking for the next five months.

During the first two weeks of nonstop talking, he burrowed his way into my life. I was so very vulnerable. I had always been sure of myself, but now I felt like a 10-year old kid who ran away from home. I had no idea what to do or what I wanted or where I was going.

So Ryan lifted my beach chair and carried me out to sea. He started commanding all my attention. We'd instant-message and video chat for hours every day. I got to know him very well, very fast.

He told me stories about his life. Ryan was named after the family dog. His parents divorced when he was young. He was close to his mom and step-dad, who lived about 20 minutes from him, but he rarely talked to his father. He had one sister who he wasn't close with. When he was in high school, he and his girlfriend had sex every day after school. He'd sit in his classroom and think, "Most of these losers probably only dream of sex! And I'm having it every. Single. Day."

He was currently married to his second wife. We'll name her Abby, a name I very much like. His first marriage to Pam ended in a bitter divorce. They had one son, and now Pam was remarried to a fat loser (his words, not mine). After he was already divorced from Pam, he met Abby at a neighborhood playground where they both brought their kids. She was stuck in an unhappy marriage but reluctant to leave because they had two kids and she had left her career behind to be a mom. Their friendship turned into a courtship of sorts. After a few months, she began taking the dogs out for a walk at 5am. She'd head straight to Ryan's house for sexy time. He hatched a plan to help her leave her miserable marriage, which included emptying bank accounts and leaving for good while her husband was at work.

Ryan was part-owner of a few homes in Colorado. He received

quarterly dividend checks from an oil well he had inherited from his grandfather. He was the co-founder of a tech startup that he was just beginning to build; he and the other co-founder had already been offered $1.8M outright for it by an un-named person. He was a skateboarder and snowboarder, hated tattoos, played the guitar, loved alternative music and was once scouted to join USA Cycling's junior/development team. Oh, and he couldn't really drink because he had contracted a form of Hepatitis at some point in his life.

If you go back and count the red flags, you'll run out of fingers. At the time, I didn't see one red flag – just a lifeline.

I only vaguely knew what he looked like, because he wasn't on Facebook. The first time we did a video chat, I was floored. He looked like one of my skater boyfriends from high school, all grown up. Tall, thin, hipster glasses, soft wavy brown hair, rings on multiple fingers, skinny jeans and Converse sneakers.

My beach chair drifted further out to sea. The coastline was a soft blur in the distance. I floated along, unable to resist.

I began waking up to long, passionate, over-the-top love letters every morning. Ryan would frantically pound out emails strewn with hyperbole and fairytales before he went to bed, when I was already sound asleep. I'd spend the first 15 or 20 minutes of my day replying. We both had rose-colored glasses firmly planted on our faces. We couldn't see anything but each other. And we soon didn't care about anything but each other.

The sneaking around began all over again. But instead of physically sneaking, I had to digitally hide my tracks. My Blackberry was never out of my hand. Weekends became excruciating, because we didn't have work to hide behind. I was once again living two lives, and I was consumed by loneliness.

E. began noticing how distant I was. I convinced him that work was consuming me. And it's true – I was incredibly busy – but only because I spent about half of every work day flirting with Ryan on video chat and NOT working. I had to catch up on real work in the evenings and on weekends. My kids, thankfully, were oblivious. Mommy was busy, end of story.

E. stepped up and took over as much kid- and household-related stuff as he could. He took the kids to the pool and the park. He took them out for ice cream and tucked them in. He made their lunches and snacks. He ran errands. He did laundry. He picked up their toys and books. He did all of this while I was busy living a double life.

***

As our conversations intensified, Ryan began complaining about Abby. She didn't like the same music as him. She read the news all the time. She had no idea what direction the Rocky Mountains were in. She burned the chicken. She hovered. She was annoying. The list went on and on.

I joined in – but of course my complaining was all about E. Complaining can be cathartic – but Ryan turned it into a weapon of destruction. Any complaint became ammunition for a full-out attack. Any flaw became an impossible-to-overcome character flaws. E. was stalled in his career? He's not aggressive enough to go after what he really wants, which means he'll always live an unfulfilled life. E. watched TV every night? He is lazy, fat and boring, which means your life with him will always be boring.

Ryan decided that I was a damsel who needed saving, and he would be my savior. I was too perfect to stay with someone like E. I had so much potential. I could live a bigger life. I could have everything I ever wanted.

And Ryan would provide it.

***

One morning, I learned what "As you wish" meant.

Ryan had been saying, "I love you." For months. It was mid-August. We had only been talking for two weeks, but he'd been saying "I love you" since May. May!

Did I love him, too? I loved all the attention, that's for sure. I loved his stories, I loved laughing with him, I loved hearing that I was beautiful and smart, and I loved feeling like I mattered.

A big wave arrived, and it pushed me even further out to sea.

"This love I feel for you … it's just overwhelming," he said during another marathon instant-message session. "I can't stop thinking about you. I dream about you all night. I think about you all day. I. Need. To. Be. With. You."

"I think about you all the time, too!" I typed back.

"I'm thinking of leaving Abby."

"WHAT?"

"I need to be with you, Monika…. I cannot live my life without you. I know it. I feel it deeply. And I can't ignore it."

"But how? We are both MARRIED."

"I love Abby, but what I feel for you … I've never felt this way before. It's insane. I know it's insane. But it's REAL."

"OMG, Ryan. I don't know what to say."

I took a deep breath. I looked out the window and then I turned towards my screen. I did know.

"I can't believe I am typing this, but I love you, Ryan. I want to be with you, too."

"What?! Do you really mean it?"

"Yes, of course I mean it silly! I wouldn't say it otherwise."

"Ohmygod, Monika. I'm shaking. You just made me the happiest human on Earth. I've never been so happy! I have never known anyone like you. I want to spend the rest of my life with you."

I began shaking. I could barely type. Now what? What am I supposed to do?

I soon got my answer: my beach chair was pushed into a fast current, and I was racing out into the open sea.

Our conversations began focusing on marriage. And building a life together. He convinced me that THIS was our future. WE were each other's future. No one else mattered. "They" would try to tear us down, because they didn't believe in it, in us, in love. But we would build a big fortress around us, and we'd be OK, because we'd be together. Happy, in love, in light, in peace. Together.

We plotted a way to meet. We lived two time zones away – he in Colorado, me in Virginia. What could we use as an excuse? We needed some sort of excuse! And then we found it. The media company we both continued to work with was holding an even in New York City in September. Perfect.

I booked a room at the W in Hoboken, NJ. He bought a plane ticket to New York. I told E. about the trip. Ryan told Abby about the trip. It was all we could talk about. But meeting once wasn't enough. Luckily, the media company was hosting events in Chicago and Denver in October. We would meet up at those too – and disguise them as work trips! We were so brilliant!

Me via IM
3 weeks…3 more weeks til we meet in person – finally! We will be kissing and laughing and crying at the airport. All at the same time. The thought of kissing you. God. I cannot wait!! It's all I think about but it can't be imagined yet. I just want to feel it not think about it.

Ryan
I know baby. It's getting more difficult each day too. It is still so impossible that we can feel this way, you know? I still can't wrap my head around it…but

I feel such an amazing connection to you that simply transcends logical explanation. How can we be so in love and never have been together?! But I know what I feel and I know it's real...if it wasn't, then how could you feel it too? Seriously...I couldn't trick you into loving me through email and text. You feel it too and I just can't explain any of it...so crazy...so wonderful.

Me
So wonderful! How will our love change when we are together? Grow stronger? I don't even try to explain it. It just is. And I am eternally grateful for you. Even though I am not religious at all, every morning when I got out for my walk, I thank god for you. Really! I love you R, with everything I am.

Ryan
And I am so grateful for you, M. I can only imagine...but I know it will grow stronger. And I know that 5 days isn't going to be enough. I don't know who to thank for you either...but whatever force has put us together I am thankful for. I love you so much M...so much more today than yesterday...with everything I am. I cannot bear the thought of you not in my life.

Me
Nor can I even think of not spending the rest of my life with you. I love you truly madly deeply, R! More today than yesterday.

***

Once again, I got sloppy. Even though this affair was conducted virtually, it was exhausting. You can only stay on high alert for so long.

It was September. Ryan and I were meeting up in a week, which meant one more week of waiting and waiting and waiting some more. Of living a double life that no longer felt like mine.

On a Sunday night, E., our kids, and I went to a concert. My life completely revolved around Ryan, and I didn't want to go. My family, my marriage and my life were obstacles standing in the way of me and Ryan being together forever. E. had purchased the concert tickets months ago. I had to go.

The entire night, I looked for quick moments to text Ryan. I was desperate for the connection and buoyancy he provided. I was completely incapable of being left on my own for too long. I never thought of it that way until now, but it's truer than true. I could not function alone. I was completely dependent on him for my sanity.

We got home late. I brought the kids up to bed and tucked them in.

I closed my daughter's bedroom door, and gasped.

"My Blackberry!" I had stupidly left it sitting on the kitchen counter.

My heart pounding, I raced down the stairs.

It was too late.

E. was reading our texts.

My heart stopped.

He knew. Oh. My. God. He knew.

I'll never forget the look on his face. The hurt, the anger, the confusion, the disappointment. It's not a look I ever want to see again.

For the next 4 ½ hours, E. and I talked. We cried, we laughed, but mostly we talked.

It was awful. My husband, the person I had fallen in love with at first sight, the father of my kids, the love of my life … was broken. I had broken him. He was crying for god's sake. He begged me to stay. He begged me to walk away from this affair. But I insisted I needed to meet Ryan. I stood my ground, and he backed down.

Finally, at 3am, I went to bed.

Ryan via email

Good morning?

I'm terrified for what you must be going through right now…I'm so sorry Monika. I know in the morning the landscape is going to be very different from what it was just an hour ago. I don't know what that will mean for us, for you, and for the future, but I just want you to know how very much I love you. I will always be here for you.

I'm not sure if it's appropriate to send the email that I had written earlier, now that things have changed drastically, I really don't know what to say, or what you want to hear.

I will be up early, I hope you were able to get some sleep.

You're my love and my life, nothing will ever change that. I love you with all that I am.

R.

Me

Good morning my love! Just going to bed. It went remarkably well. I feel so much better - a huge burden has lifted that's for sure. So I am getting divorced, but we talked for like 4 1/2 hours and it was very agreeable and amicable all around. He knows about you but only a bit. I told him that I think there is something here (as in you and I). We will talk more tomorrow. I am so fucking tired I need a few hours of sleep before I am delirious.

I love you baby; things have changed but only for the better.

XO from your little pixie,
M.

Me

Good morning - again - but this time after 3 hours of sleep. Last night was surreal - surreal! I can't believe he read some of our texts - not enough to get the full pic, but still. There is much to tell you, that's for sure.

But now I am moving forward and though last night was not easy, it was not total hell either. We were laughing a lot actually. But he agrees that the kids are our #1 priority, and we will work out the financial aspect. We even started dividing up what I get to take - in terms of our artwork, etc.

He saw it coming, but was still shocked. Of course. This is what he knows about us: that we are very close and talk a lot, that you offered me a job that is a once in a lifetime opportunity, and that there is possibly something - some future - between you and I.

So I will fill you in more later. I don't know what time he is going to work - late this morning. Will keep you posted. I am so sorry I went dark so abruptly. I wanted to text or call you but could not til 3am, and I was really upset I could not somehow let you know that things were ok.

I love you R., more than you will ever know.

XO,
M.

Him

Good morning, love of my life…my gorgeous M.!

Today started sort of low and slow, with the hangover from your awful night…a night that you'll have a hard time remembering, but will never forget. I want to say again how incredibly proud of you I am. Every day you amaze me, but what you did, and how you handled it and the shit storm that followed was brave and courageous and took so much strength and poise. You're such an inspiration to me…on so many levels. It's wonderful to be proud of the woman you love, and I have so much respect for you…you are constantly giving me new reasons to be grateful for you. And I am so very, very grateful that you are not just a part of my life, but that you ARE my life.

I simply can't wait for next week…baby, we're just 5 days away, and I am so excited for the weekend at the beach! Wow - how exciting…god, we really truly are going to live a lifetime next week. I just can't even imagine the time we're going to have…it will be heavenly, that's the best I can come up with. I can honestly say this: if we didn't have sex one single time, I wouldn't care…if all I could do was be next to you, share the same space as you…and kiss you, it

33

would have the greatest week of my life. Just to feel your hand in mine will be a dream come true…and knowing what will come after that…OMG BABY!

So here's the bit I wrote for you last night…

One of the things I love hearing from you is that early on you were sort of interested in me, but you figured that nothing would come of it. What with the distance and the possibility of ever even MEETING in person - it would be interesting, but probably never going to happen. I LOVE hearing you say that, because I never doubted it would happen. I never for a second thought about the distance or the remote possibilities of seeing you in person, of spending time getting to know you, or the fact that you were married. None of it. None of it ever occurred to me. And what I love about that, is that it's completely insane that it never occurred to me…completely! What the hell!? Seriously…there's no logical explanation for why those things never entered my head. I never had any doubt, never had any thoughts of failure…I never EVER doubted for a second that we would be where we are today. And that is just plain crazy…I've never felt anything like it… the pull to you, towards "us." Like I was the Terminator with this preprogramed message in my head compelling me towards you. And that's the word that I thought of this morning…compelled. There's no question we are connected, but there's also no question that we've always been connected… in the past, in the future, who knows, how time really works…or what this plane of existence really means. All I know is this: when I think of you, there is this piece of it that I can only call "certainty." That you are the one that completes me, the one I SHOULD be with…the one I've been compelled to find. Once I allowed myself to listen…to hear you calling me, to BE pulled, I never, ever doubted the outcome…and it is simply fucking amazing. The odds, the distance, the obstacle — it's just so ridiculous to even imagine. Yet, here we are, against all possible odds, we are we, and in less than a week, we'll finally become "us."

I want you to know this: today my love for you grew 10 times over. You have changed overnight, and I love this new you more than I'll ever have words to describe, and it was just so fucking nice to be with you…to share the day. You and I will have the life that dreams are made of…that movies are made of…the stuff of fairytales. I don't know if ever felt it so strongly as I did today, as I do now…but nothing makes me happier to think about our future together. We are we, and in 5 days, we'll have the week of our lives and will become us.

I love you M., with all that I have and all that I am.

XOXO

-R.

Chapter 3

Reality Bites

My life was completely warped. I no longer recognized my husband. My marriage felt fake. My sweet, darling children were a nuisance. My reality was on shaky ground. Everything and everyone was now an obstacle. I was destroying my life, and I was helpless to stop it.

I didn't know who I was anymore. My entire identity was defined by and entangled with Ryan's. Our relationship had consumed me. Ryan got what he wanted – me. I got – emptiness.

Of course, I see this clearly now. But when you're in the middle of everything – when you are living a warped reality – delusions and illusions weave a complex, invisible web around your life. And then they strangle it.

***

Finally, the day had arrived. It was time to meet Ryan.

After the volcanic build-up, the anguished texts, the emails filled with violent desire, the obsessive video chats, we would finally be face-to-face.

It was a brilliant Sunday morning. It was also the morning after E.'s and my 11th wedding anniversary. I was anxious bordering on hysterical. I used every ounce of energy I had to act cool. I didn't want to rub it in E.'s face. He knew exactly what I was about to do – and he knew I didn't care.

I went for a walk, made coffee, finished packing my suitcase and sat down in front of my computer. I didn't know what else to do anymore but work – or at least hide behind work. While I distracted myself, E. gathered up the kids, filled their water bottles and ushered them out the door. He was bringing them to his pick-up soccer game, where they would be happily distracted playing with friends. Mommy was going on a business trip, and they'd see me in a week.

E. played it cool, too. But inside he was crumbling. He couldn't look at me as he turned and closed the door behind him.

I looked around our empty house. The silence and sadness were excruciating. I trudged up the stairs and stood in my son's doorway. I looked at his Legos and stuffed bear and his little socks balled up on the floor. The heaviness grew.

Then I walked down the hall and looked in my daughter's room, where I had been sleeping for a month. Her dolls were lined up in a row, cheerfully sitting where she had left them yesterday. Her hair ties and sunglasses were piled on her dresser. I sat on her bed. The heaviness was weighing on me.

I got up and walked across the hall to our bedroom, where E. had tearfully spent the last month, alone. The room looked foreign to me. I felt ... nothing.

"I need to get out of here," I thought.

I walked down the hall, gathered my things, hoisted my bags in the trunk and drove off to live a week-long, fucked up, and completely twisted fairytale.

I tried not to speed, but I did. I raced up I-95 through Maryland, Delaware, and New Jersey. The weather was perfect. The traffic was non-existent. And in a blink of an eye, I was pulling into a parking lot at Newark Airport. I was calm as can be, as if it was perfectly normal to drive through three states to meet a man who I knew only virtually, but who I found myself completely dependent upon for every shred of happiness.

Even when I walked through the terminal doors at Newark, I didn't feel nervous. I found Ryan's gate and sat down. I opened up the latest issue of Food & Wine Magazine and read it cover to cover.

I looked at the time. Almost 2pm. His flight lands in 30 minutes. I looked at the arrivals board – still on time.

At 2pm, I started pacing the airport.

At 2:30, Ryan texted, "I'm here!"

I flipped out. I could barely stand still. I leaned up against the glass railing, directly opposite of where I knew he would emerge from his flight. I stared straight ahead, ready.

Passengers slowly emerged one-by-one. Then a family walked into the terminal, followed by another. Then four businessmen – all on their phones – appeared in a clump.

And suddenly, there he was, right in front of me, smiling from ear to ear.

The world stood still.

I couldn't breathe. Everyone faded into the background. All I could see was Ryan.

He was standing right there. Right in front of me. Right where he was meant to be.

I was in shock. He is here! Oh. My. God. He. Is. Here.

It was go-time.

I don't remember how I got to him, but I did. We staggered into each other's arms. We were finally touching, and it was fucking surreal. I opened my mouth to say hi, but nothing came out. Ryan was shaking. He wrapped me in a bear hug me. "It's you!" he said. "It's you! You're here!"

I was wrapped up in the arms of the man who upended my life. At that moment, I loved him more than anything in the world. He was my sole reason for being, my other half, the only person in the world who understood me and appreciated me. After all that time, after a lifetime of walking towards each other, we were finally we.

"Yes, it's me!" I gasped. "It's me! And you're you!"

We had to sit down. We were both completely overwhelmed. Neither of us could stop grinning. We couldn't stop touching each other, either, and we definitely couldn't stop staring.

Once we regained our composure, we took the escalator downstairs, grabbed his luggage from the baggage carousel, walked to my car, and set off for the W in Hoboken.

The next week was a complete blur. I spent so much of my time trying to burrow into him, where I would be safe and protected and no one could find us. I was so desperate for some sense of security, something to hold onto, something that would just stop moving so I could be still and relax and BREATHE for the first time in months.

And if you must ask, yes, the sex was out of this world. What do you expect from months of flirting and weeks of daily, over-the-top, bodice-ripping love letters?

Being with Ryan was exactly what I expected. Ryan in reality was the same person as Ryan in virtual reality. He was completely focused on me and us, and he was as surprised as I was that we had pulled this little stunt off. My spouse knew exactly what was happening. His spouse was suspicious and jumpy and upset. But who cares? E. and Abby didn't matter. We mattered, because we were we.

That first night together, we went for a walk along the Hudson River. The magical Manhattan skyline shimmered, and the gorgeous energy of the city pulsated out to us across the water. Ryan toted along his camera and took photos of me, a blissful fool who looked gobsmacked by mix of happiness, surprise and exhaustion.

For a week, we slept entwined in each other. It felt so natural, so normal, so cozy. As we'd drift off, we'd declare our undying love for each other. Every night, he whispered, "I will never, ever let you go. You are mine, and I am yours, and we are we." I'd smile and sleep dreamless nights.

Contrary to our actions, we were not on vacation. We both needed to work, though it was the last thing I wanted to do. I had been addicted to a screen for months, using it as my lifeline. Now my lifeline was right here next to me, and I wanted to just *be*.

On Wednesday, we finally left our hotel bunker. We wandered down the sidewalk, giggling like preschoolers who had just stolen our teacher's stash of M&Ms, and headed into Manhattan.

Our first stop was Tiffany's. Of course. We'd already gone too far – why not push it over the edge? We stepped into the cool, dark foyer and headed for the wide staircase. We practically ran up to the second floor. A salesman spotted us mooning over each other and immediately walked over to greet us. His name was Tony, and he and Ryan chatted away about carats and clarity and cut and color. Ryan knew a lot about fine jewelry – much more than I did. After about 10 minutes, Tony and Ryan were new best friends. I just stood there, grinning my foolish face off. Ryan picked out my engagement ring and wedding band as Tony dutifully wrote down all the details on his business card. We shook hands, said our good-byes and practically floated back down the wide staircase.

As the sun hit our faces and the tourists on Fifth Avenue surged around us, Ryan turned to me and declared, "I am going to get you a third ring. It will be to show you – and the entire fucktard world – how much truly madly deeply I love you."

Wow. I was floored. Who does that? Ryan! Of course. If it's over-the-top, it's Ryan.

We walked a couple of blocks up Fifth Avenue and ducked into the late, great FAO Schwartz to get gifts for my kids. Then we did the next logical thing and went to … Barney's, the temple of luxury where you want everything and need nothing. "You know what we need?" Ryan asked, a big sloppy grin on his face.

"What?"

"New fragrances," he declared. "We need fragrances that are only for each other. No one else. Not E. Not Abby. For us."

So we marched right over to the men's fragrance counter. We – and by we, I mean I – dropped a boatload of cash on Byredo products. We spritzed and sniffed til our noses gave out. I fell in love with Bal D'Afrique. Ryan settled on Number 2. "Perfect!" we said. "They smell like us."

Where to next? We stood on Madison Avenue facing north. "I think it's about six blocks up this way," I said, "to the JCrew Bridal Boutique."

We walked hand-in-hand up the street. Cabs and black Mercedes sedans and a skateboarder passed us as we walked in the shadow of the skyscraper canyon. We finally found ourselves standing in front of the jewel box-sized JCrew Bridal. "Oh man!" I complained. "Stupid place is by appointment only!"

"That's OK," Ryan reassured me. "We can still go in and look around. You don't need an appointment for looking. Or do you?"

"I don't know!" I replied. "Let's go in and find out!"

We opened the door and were immediately surrounded by fluffy white dresses. We were free to look around – or so I think, since no one bothered us.

The fourth dress I looked at was The One. It was perfect for a beach wedding.

By now it was getting rainy and late and it was time to head downtown. The media company was throwing an event that night at General Assembly. We had to go – we had to be in the photos – because that event was our flimsy excuse for being in New York.

We took a cab downtown to Gramercy Tavern, hoping to snag a last-minute table for two. Never underestimate the need for restaurant reservations in New York – they had a two-hour wait at 6pm! On a Wednesday! We ducked into CraftBar next door instead.

And then it was show time. We walked the few rainy blocks to General Assembly, where we chatted, flirted and held hands. After an hour, it was time to retreat. We'd been out of our bunker for far too long.

The next morning, we slept in, worked reluctantly and once again giggled all the way into the city. Our agenda today was different: sexy underwear. Ryan was aghast that I was not outfitted like a Victoria's Secret Angel. Once again, we – and by we, I mean I – dropped a boatload of money at the Victoria's Secret in Herald Square. Ryan ran around the store, picking out the skimpiest, laciest, craziest get-ups he could find. He was like a hormone-fueled teenager, and I merrily went along.

Back out on the sidewalk, gigantic pink-and-white striped bag in hand, we headed to a meeting at the Ace Hotel with the owners of the media company. The lobby was gloomy, frigid and filled with hipsters painfully hunched over Macbooks. I couldn't wait to get out of there and defrost and have Ryan all to myself again. Reality kept butting in, and I wanted it gone – for good.

On a gray Friday morning, we checked out of the W and drove south – to the beach. We picked Belmar, an old-school Jersey shore town, as our new hideout. A small B&B in an ancient farmhouse became our bunker. For three mostly cloudy days, we ignored work and talked obsessively about our future. How would this – "we" – work? Where would we live? When could we marry? Where would we get married? How would Ryan tell Abby? What about the kids? How would custody work? What kind of house would we live in? Where would we spend vacations and holidays? When would his startup launch, and how much revenue would be coming in? How rich would we be? Could we retire early? Where would we travel? How would we build the perfect life that we had always wanted?

During one semi-sunny afternoon, we carried beach chairs, towels and a library's worth of shelter catalogues to the beach. As we flipped through West Elm, Pottery Barn, Crate & Barrel, Restoration Hardware, Frontgate and Williams-Sonoma, we picked out our favorite furniture and placed them in imaginary rooms in our imaginary house. We designed our kitchen, family room, living room, and bedroom. We styled our dining table and outdoor living areas. We discussed the merits of white towels and white dishes and the need for a heated salt-water swimming pool.

On our last night, we ate dinner in a nearly-deserted restaurant overlooking a channel that connected the ocean to the bay. A sad, rusted-out fishing boat sat half-sunk into the sludge across the channel from our romantic table for two. Our tired waiter shuffled about, setting down plates and glasses absent-mindedly. It was a quiet, forlorn scene, and Ryan and I were quiet. The next day, our trip was over. Reality would return, and neither of us were prepared for it.

Monday was hot and muggy, and we were damp with sweat as we slowly packed my car. The drive back to Newark was depressing. We kept reminding each other that we'd be together again in Chicago soon – but we couldn't convince ourselves that the time between now and then would go quickly or that re-entry into our lives would be easy. I could not cheer him up, nor him I. My god, I did not want to re-enter the real world. I didn't even know what the real world was anymore. Was it this, or was it the smoldering wreck at home? I felt punched in the gut, unable to catch my breath, and once we got to the airport, the tears wouldn't stop. Neither of us could hold it together. Ryan looked absolutely wrecked. I'm sure I looked worse.

"Chicago is only 2 ½ weeks away," he kept saying. "It's where it had all started, and it will be amazing. It'll be perfect. It'll be different than New York – but better." I willed myself to believe him.

Then I turned and walked away. I walked down the escalator, through the terminal, and through the parking lot to my car. I felt empty.

On my drive home, I called my parents. It all spilled out – the breakdown in my marriage, what I had just been doing in New York, who I was with, what my plans were. To say they were shocked would be a gross understatement, but I am still in awe of their compassionate response. They listened with patience and love, and they asked a lot of questions. They gave me space to express what I needed to say and didn't try to argue with me.

Over the next week, this conversation played out multiple times.

One by one, I called my brothers. Then I called my closest friends. Then I called my aunt and two uncles. The reaction was always the same: shock, followed by questions. The conversations never got easier.

E. did the same. He called his parents, his sister, his extended family and his close friends. But then he did something I did not – he called my friends. And he started digging into who this Ryan guy was. He needed to know who he was up against.

As the news spread, we lost friends. Our best friends stood by us, of course, but many other friends distanced themselves or completely disappeared. There was a lot of whispering and snickering and speculation behind our backs. I can only imagine the things that were said about me. But I didn't care. I was in love, and I was going to live a bigger, better life. We were going to build a company together! Ryan was going to cash in some investments to give us a big, fat, financial cushion of fun money. We were going to travel all over the world and we were going to be the happiest motherfuckers on the planet. Life was going to be one big rose-colored, confetti-sprinkled party, and we were going to be in the middle of it.

E. and I decided to tell our kids what was happening. They were so little and sweet and filled with love, but it had to be done. Our daughter was in third grade and our son was in kindergarten. We gathered in our son's room before bed one night, and sat on the floor.

"Daddy and I are not happy," I began, "and we are going to separate. I am going to move out, and you will stay here with Daddy. But you will live with me, too. Every other week."

Our son's crumpled in a heap, inconsolable. Our daughter burst into tears and hugged us. I destroyed their happy little lives, because I was a selfish asshole.

***

On Tuesday, October 11, I popped out of bed at 5am. It was pitch black and unusually warm as I stepped outside and into the cab. The flight to Chicago was quick and easy, but I was in excruciating pain. My right shoulder had seized up on me, and now I felt like a knife was sticking out of it. All my stress had zeroed in on this one part of my exhausted body, a constant reminder of the mess I had become.

After grabbing a quick breakfast at Starbuck's, I headed straight from O'Hare to the historic Drake Hotel. When I was told our room was ready and I could check in at 10am, I took it as a sign that this would be another perfect and magical visit with my love. I floated over to the elevator bank, stared into the dreamy distance on the elevator ride up and practically skipped down the hall to our room. Et voila – we had a gorgeous view of the mighty Lake Michigan – another sign. And my god, that lake was so blue. It was truly an exquisite neighbor.

Now it was time to wait again. I grabbed my Mac and went downstairs to the lobby, where I bought an hour's worth of Wi-Fi and worked. I waited somewhat patiently for Ryan to appear and rescue me. When he texted that his cab was about 10 minutes away, I began anxiously looking up whenever someone walked by. By now, I was weary of waiting. My entire life had turn into a waiting room. I was waiting to hear from Ryan, waiting to see him again, waiting to move out of my house, waiting to start my picture-perfect forever life with Ryan.

Then I looked up, and there he was, walking slowly up the lobby steps with the biggest shit-eating grin on his face. Look what we were getting away with – AGAIN!

I practically chucked my Mac across the lobby in my rush to him. We hugged so tightly – so very tightly. I needed to absorb him again. I needed to feel safe and protected and loved. I needed to hide.

We were both bursting with excitement. Since getting home from New York, I had been working on his birthday present, which was coming up in two weeks. It was a book I self-published. Unbeknownst to Ryan, I had been saving our messages to each other. It began with a text message on August 22 and faithfully followed our trail of insanity. Emails, texts and IMs were all in there. Our bad behavior was bound in a book for posterity – and it was his birthday present.

"Sit down and close your eyes," I instructed.

He sat down on the ornate bed and closed his eyes, a big smile still plastered on his face. I pulled the book out of my suitcase and held it up in front of him. "Ok, open them!"

Ryan looked confused. "It's a book?"

"Yes! It's the story of us," and I explained my little project to him as he flipped through the pages.

"Oh my god," he said. "No one has ever given me a gift like this. No one!" He pulled me into his arms, wrapping me up in the book, in him, in us. He looked up at me. "I love it, Monika. Thank you so much – this is truly the best gift I have ever received. I will always treasure it."

Our magical moment complete, now it was time for Ryan to show me what he had been planning. But first, lunch! We grabbed a late lunch in one of the Drake's restaurants before embarking on what Ryan called the Monika Tour on the Magnificent Mile. Ryan wanted to show me every single spot from his trip to Chicago in July that was somehow connected to us.

First stop: Nordstrom. Ryan had first texted and then called me in July from outside Nordstrom. We sat in one chair. "This is where I was sitting when I texted you." Then we moved to another chair. "This is where I called you from." I clearly remembered that phone call. I didn't know what to think or why he reached out to me, but I was so glad he did. That confusion had given way to clarity. I didn't know he was trying his darndest to turn me around to REALLY see him – but now I knew.

The tour continued as we walked to the Chicago River. It was here that Ryan took a photo of the sunset in July, when it was so god awful hot out and he could not stop thinking about me. In the lead-up to our Chicago trip, he had sent it to me, and now it was the background image on my Mac, a constant reminder of "us".

On our walk back to the Drake, I saw The Purple Pig. I had read about it when I was waiting for Ryan's flight to arrive in Newark. Another sign! We had a drink and a phenomenal dinner before returning to our new hideout where no one could touch us, where we could be us.

Wednesday was another gorgeous day. We slept in, but I had to jump out of bed, throw on a sweater, and do a video chat with the kids before they went to school. I had promised them we would, and I nearly forgot about it.

By now, my shoulder was almost immobile. I could barely stand the pain. "Monika, you need a massage," Ryan declared. "Call the concierge – they'll tell you where to go." I booked a massage at a spa one block away. Sweet relief! My shoulder wasn't 100%, but I could move it without wincing.

I returned to the hotel to find Ryan working in bed, delighted to have me back. I had to do some work too, and I turned to him and said, "As much as I love to work, it seems like such a waste of time when I am with you – like it just does … not … matter – only you do."

"Oh baby. I feel the same way," he replied. The love in his eyes just washed over me, and I relaxed as I sunk back into the pillows.

Because the weather was supposed to be crappy the next day, we dined al fresco at a small Italian café and went for a nice long walk. We meandered down the Magnificent Mile until we reached Grant Park. I so wanted to see the bench that Ryan sat on during that hot July night – when he just knew there was some cosmic force at work, pulling him toward me. "It's at least another mile or two away. I don't really want to walk that far," Ryan insisted.

Instead, we walked around a marina and gazed up at the extremely tall building where his grandparents had lived when he was little. We sat on a bench facing it, and Ryan told me stories about spending time with them on school breaks. They were very rich and very distant. He had fond memories of Chicago but not really of them.

On our walk back to the Drake, Ryan stopped at a Jamba Juice for a smoothie. On our way out, he stopped in his tracks. "Holy crap," he said. "I went to this same Jamba Juice back in July in the blazing heat! I was missing you so much, and I just needed to cool off. Here we are, at yet another stop on the Monika Tour!"

We laughed as we walked back up the newly renamed Magnificent Marvelous Monika Mile. Ryan half-whispered, "All the guys are seriously checking you out."

"No, they're not – don't be ridiculous."

"Oh but they are – just look!"

I watched the faces of all the men we walked past. Whether they were in business suits or jeans, sure enough – they were all stealing a glance or outright gaping! I couldn't believe it. I still didn't think I was that much to look at – but Ryan turned to me and said, "Of course they are staring. You are the most beautiful woman in the world."

Our feet were aching from all the walking, so we revived ourselves with Manhattans in The Drake's beautiful bar. We cozied up in a love seat, safe and sound in our perfect togetherness. We were we, and we were still safe and sound.

We woke up to a rainy Thursday and spent the morning working. After lunch, we went to a super-chic mall across the street. The mall happened to house a JCrew Bridal Boutique. We picked out two dresses for me to try on – the one I really liked in NYC and another called the Lucinda. When I put on the Lucinda, Ryan's face lit up like the noonday sun.

"It's perfect!" he said. "You look … so … perfect."

We loved it so much, and we loved our salesgirl so much, that I went ahead and bought the dress right then and there. Because putting a $2,700 charge on your credit card while in another city with your lover is a great idea. Naturally, sirens went off at the credit card company. They called E., despite the fact that I was the primary account holder. E. called me immediately, livid. Absolutely livid.

"What the hell are you spending money on?" he yelled as soon as I answered.

"Oh, um …" I stalled. I had no idea what to say. "I went on a little shopping spree at JCrew," I feebly replied.

"Little? LITTLE? How is $2,700 little?"

"Um. I don't know. I guess I bought a lot of stuff."

"Oh, really? Like what? A wedding dress?"

How did he know? Jesus Christ, how did he know?

I had just thrown fuel on an already raging fire. I could have avoided this by charging the dress to my business credit card. Or, you know, NOT doing something so stupid.

I was so upset. Ryan tried to cheer me up, but no matter what I said, I was so pissed at myself. I was getting reckless. I was getting sloppy. It was not good.

That night, Ryan felt ill. We had just finished a fabulous dinner when Ryan declared he was dizzy and didn't feel right. What had started off as a great day just kept going downhill. Our magical, perfect time together was turning out to be not so magical or perfect anymore. Real life was pushing its way into our bunker.

Friday was a new day, though. The sun was out and so was the wind. After a good night's sleep, we'd behave much more reasonably today. And by reasonably, that meant going to the local David Yurman store. They handed us flutes of champagne as we browsed men's rings. We had already picked my rings out at Tiffany's, so it only made sense that we pick out a ring for Ryan. I had already done some reconnaissance with a friend at home, so I knew which one I liked. Of course, Ryan loved it too. It was from their Waves collection, and because it was reasonably priced (remember, we were being reasonable today), I bought it for him, this time using my business credit card.

"You know I can't bring the ring home with me," Ryan said as we walked back to The Drake. "If Abby finds this, she will freak the fuck out. She's already on edge – this will push her over it."

"Don't worry, I'll bring it home with me. E. will never even know to look for it," I reassured him.

And it was true – about Abby anyway. She pretty much knew what was going on. She was hovering over him whenever he was on the computer, asking roundabout questions about me, asking pointed questions about our work together, and trying to explain everything away. Ryan said he just nodded and agreed with her. She had begun floating the idea of an open marriage to him. When he told me during one of our daily video chats, I snorted with laughter.

"That's so ridiculous," I said.

"Well, if it gets her off my back and stops her from snooping, I'm fine with it," Ryan replied. And I kind of agreed with that logic, but I had to constantly remind myself that everything would work out. Once I was home from Chicago, I occasionally took Ryan's ring out of the box and put it on my finger, willing myself to believe that one day soon we would be together forever.

Our Chicago trip was so much different than our giddy NYC trip. We weren't as relaxed as we were in NYC. Not only did we work a lot more, we were both stressed about work. I tried to convince myself it was because this was a much shorter trip, but it was our irresponsibility.

Reality stormed back into our lives on Saturday. It was time to pack and go home. I took cab out to Midway with Ryan, as my flight was not leaving from O'Hare til that night. Finding a quiet place to sit was not easy. We ended up next to an empty luggage carousel and cuddled like lovesick teenagers. I had to absorb him before our good-bye.

As I drove in the cab back to Chicago, I felt empty once again. I went for a walk, but the more I walked, the sadder I felt. I was unmoored – just a sad, lonely person in her beach chair, floating in the middle of the ocean. I was all alone. No one could see me, and I didn't even know if anyone was looking for me. If someone had found me, would they have been able to help me? Doubtful. I looked up the intricate façade of an old-money townhouse along the Gold Coast. Were the people who lived here sad – or happy? Would I ever be happy again? I was beginning to doubt … everything.

When I couldn't take it anymore, I went back to The Drake, fetched my luggage, and cabbed it to O'Hare. I made one last stop on the Monika Tour – the Wolfgang Puck restaurant. Ryan had eaten there before flying home to Denver from Chicago in July. I looked at the people sitting around the bar. Ryan had sat on one of those barstools, unable to stop thinking about me. Now all I could think about what Denver. I was flying there in two short weeks.

***

Ryan was beyond excited to introduce me to his hometown. He had everything planned: One night in Vail, two nights in Boulder, and one night in Denver. It would be … perfect.

And the trip was perfect – at first. Because work was my haven, I plowed through one project after another during my flight west. Time moved so quickly on the flight that we landed 20 minutes early. I gazed out the window, transfixed by the snow-capped Rocky Mountains in the distance. "My god, they are so gorgeous," I thought. "I can't wait to live out here."

I texted Ryan that I had arrived. He called. "Wow – that was a fast flight! Listen, I'm still about 40 minutes away. Abby called right after I left to let me know I forgot my computer bag. The crazy things is, I knew I had packed it the night before!"

"That is crazy," I said, "Well, I bet she took it out and went through it, looking for something."

"Mmm, that's not really like her," he hedged. "With her new open marriage plan, she basically leaves me alone. But in any case, I'm on my way, and I'll see you very, very soon my sweet little pixie Monika!"

"Aww, love it when you call me that," I cooed into the phone. "I missed you so much – I can't wait to see you! I'll call you once I have my suitcase, and you can just tell me where to meet you."

Before I even got to baggage claim area, he called. I knew something was wrong. And it was. His truck (a BMW X5, not really a truck-truck) had broken down 15 minutes from the airport. Some asshole had zoomed by him in a pickup truck – "He was going at least 100mph!" – and Ryan ran over a piece of metal that flew out of the back of the pickup. He didn't have a flat tire, but the engine was damaged. He was mad as hell and beginning to panic.

The solution was obvious: I'll rent a car. While Ryan was waiting for a tow truck, I hustled over to the first rental car company I saw and snagged some random Chevy SUV thing. It was ugly as hell, but it didn't matter. We had wheels. He told me what exit he was near, and when I arrived, there was his truck, up on the back of a flat bed, ready to be towed. I had barely put the car in park before I jumped out of the car and into his arms. I was home.

We headed straight to Vail. Along the way, he pointed out Ryan-specific landmarks. "Here's my exit, there's where my parents live, I used to play golf there."

The drive into the mountains was gorgeous. I took pictures of Keystone and Copper – both resorts already had some snow – and marveled at the perfect weather. Clear blue skies, abundant sunshine, and tempereatures in the 70s. I was so excited to be in Colorado, and the perfect weather reflected my mood.

We stopped at the tiny old town of Idaho Springs for lunch. The Cowboys game was on. Ryan was a huge fan, so we couldn't leave til the game was over. He kept apologizing, but honestly, I didn't care much. I only cared that we were together. I moved to his side of the booth and give the evil eye to the teenybopper who had been checking him out. I had never felt possessive of anyone – ever – but I felt like I had to plant my flag on him. He found it all rather amusing.

The closer we got to Vail, the more excited Ryan became. It was one of his favorite places in the world, and he couldn't wait to share it with me. We checked into the cutest little hotel and went for a walk. I was stunned by not only how gorgeous Vail was, but how Bavarian it was. It was as if someone had plopped a Bavarian Alpine village in Colorado. Streets were narrow and cobblestoned, the architecture was definitely Bavarian and many businesses had German names.

I loved it. I felt like I was home, and not just because I was with Ryan. There was something very comfortable and familiar about Vail.

We woke up on Monday to some very, very cold weather – crystal clear skies and about 30 degrees. We had breakfast just down the street at Ludwig's at the Sonnenalp. Ryan knew I would love it, and he was right. He watched my reaction as I walked through the hotel to the restaurant. The hotel was insanely elegant. "My god, I love it here!" I gasped. He smiled knowingly – of course I loved it here. He did too. During breakfast, Ryan floated the idea of buying a fractional share so we'd have a home away from home in the mountains.

The fantasy continued that afternoon as soon as we walked through the doors of Gorsuch. I don't even know how to describe this store on Teutonic steroids, other than it's a luxury retailer of Bavarian and Austrian products that you don't need but you most definitely want. Need a bespoke dirndl? Go to Gorsuch. Need a heavy woolen jacket with wooden buttons? Go to Gorsuch. Need beautifully embroidered linens? Gorsuch.

I totally fell in love with Vail, and I couldn't wait to go back and snowboard in a few months.
As we drove away, I felt like I was leaving my new best friend. But adventure awaited! On to Boulder!

As we zoomed down I-70, chatting away, Ryan spotted a cop car – but it was too late to hit the brakes. We were pulled over, and unfortunately, the cop was in a non-charitable mood. Ryan received both a speeding ticket and a citation for driving with an expired license (which he knew about but pretended he didn't). Now he had to appear in court on December 23. The mood turned from jubilant to angry. I tried to cheer him up, but reality was once again shoving its way into our perfect fantasy world. And it sucked.

That evening, we had to make an appearance at the media company's event in Boulder – it was our excuse – yet again – for being together. Despite having to share our time together with other people, we had fun. We grabbed a late dinner at a brewery next door with two of the developers who were working with Ryan on that big startup – remember that? – the one that would make us millionaires? After hearing about them for months, it was nice to put a face to a name.

Reality intervened once again on Tuesday morning. We both had tons of work to do, because as usual we were slacking off and having fun. A huge storm was bearing down on Denver, so I had to change my flight home from tomorrow afternoon to first thing in the morning. I had found an apartment to move into on November 1 – so soon! – and I had a shit-ton of furniture to order from IKEA, which took forever.

We also found something missing that morning. Ryan was rummaging through his computer bag, growing agitated, and finally declared, "SHIT!"

"What's wrong honey?"

"I know what Abby was doing with my computer bag on Saturday night."

"Oh god, what now?"

"See this folder?" And he held up a plain manila folder with no markings on it – just a paper clip attached to it.

"Yes … ?"

"So, remember I told you the dividend check had arrived last week?"

"Ohmigod – she took it!"

"She sure did. Shit, shit, shit!"

One of the many things Ryan had told me about himself – if you recall – is that he owned shares in some oil company. He got a quarterly dividend check, and normally he just turned it over to Abby. Well, the plan was to hide it from her, bring it with him so we could cash it, and pay me back for all the expenses I had incurred during our New York and Chicago trips.

I said, "Well, she was looking for something, and she found it."

Before we left Boulder, we stopped for lunch. Already the weather was changing from warm and sunny to overcast and cold. Ryan gave me an abbreviated driving tour of UC Boulder – where he had gone to college – and then we drove into Denver. As we drove, a sense of dread washed over me. It was such a short trip, everything seemed rushed, and the crazy morning left me feeling even more vulnerable and exposed than usual. I had been racking up debt to pay for our trips, and I had just spent a few thousand dollars at IKEA. Ryan had promised to reimburse me for everything. That check was supposed to be for me – for us – for our new life – and now it was gone.

We drove into downtown Denver and walked around for a bit. Oddly enough, Ryan walked me over to an empty sidewalk in front of a restaurant and proceeded to tell me a story. Ryan used to be a completely different person – that I knew. During his first marriage, he worked nonstop in finance. He wore a suit to work every day, drove a flashy BMW and was completely dedicated to making money. He was fat and out of shape and completely miserable.

One day, he was having drinks after work with his buddies, sitting outside on the restaurant's terrace. The waitress was hot – but not hotter than me, he was quick to point that out – and she was funny and lovely and smart. He thought, "What the fuck am I doing? I need to get out of this stupid life." He pursued this waitress like his life depended on it. He moved out of his house and into an apartment with her. They decamped to Mexico for a few months, until he came to his senses. He moved back home and begged his wife to take him back. She did. They went to counseling, worked things out and stayed together for a few more years.

But that experience – of following his bliss – had changed him. He ditched the suits and corporate life. He started working out and skateboarding again. He pursued graphic design but still randomly traded stocks for fun. He began listening to alternative rock and playing the guitar again.

He changed who he was completely – and he was no longer the person his first wife had married. They divorced.

As he told me this story, I was both amused and confused. Amused, because this is where he began turning into the person who was standing beside me. Confused, because now I wondered if I was just his next waitress. There was a pattern here. Pursue a gorgeous, amazing woman like a crazy person. Upend both your life and hers. Retreat to safety, leaving behind plenty of wreckage.

Was he going to retreat and leave me out in the ocean by myself?

I wouldn't – I couldn't – believe it. We'd come so far together. We were we. He and I were meant for each other. He said he'd never ever let me go. He loved me like he'd never loved anyone else.

No. This was different – I wasn't just "some" waitress. I was his little pixie, and everything would be fine.

The wind was picking up and it was getting cold. The sun had disappeared and the beautiful weather we had enjoyed over the last two days was a distant memory. We walked back to our car, where we found a parking ticket. We forgot to feed the meter.

"God, what could happen next?" Ryan remarked. We both laughed it off, but what happened next was not funny.

We checked into a super crappy hotel at the airport. It was so worn out and sad that it verged on depressing. Ryan said he tried the Ritz-Carlton in town, but it was booked for some lawyer convention. It was raining when we drove back into Denver for dinner. After dinner, the rain began transitioning to snow.

At 5:15 the next morning, the alarm Ryan set on his phone went off. He had set it "just in case" right after we set the alarm on the bedside clock. The hotel clock alarm never went off. I took a quick shower, we packed our stuff, and Ryan asked for the car keys so he could pull the rental car around. "I don't have them! You do!"

"Monika, I gave you the keys last night!"

"Well, they're not in my purse."

We turned the hotel room and all our luggage inside out. Ryan called the front lobby - no one had turned them in. There was three inches of snow on the ground and it was dark outside, so it was impossible to see anything in the parking lot. At this point, it was almost 6am, and I had a 7:20am flight.

I was panicked – beyond panicked.

At 6:05am we boarded a shuttle bus to the airport. We said our goodbyes quickly at security and kept reminding each other that our separation was temporary. Ryan would be in DC in two weeks! Just two weeks. We could make it through yet another separation. I hugged Ryan as tight as I could before I walked away. After I breezed through security, I turned and waved.

That was the last time I saw him.

And you know what? When I turned and walked towards my gate, I knew. I knew it was over.

***

One week after arriving home from Denver, I moved out of my house and into an apartment. I was a ball of anxiety, bouncing all over the place but never settling. "I'll be there soon!" Ryan said. "And then all of this – all the stress, all the worry – will be over. One day, it'll be over and we'll be together forever." I could barely sleep or eat or function, but his reassurances kept me moving forward.

Two and half months of putting up with my ridiculous and utterly foreign behavior had taken its toll on E. By the time I moved out, he had disengaged from me entirely. It was the only way he kept his sanity, managed the kids and accomplished anything at work. He surrounded himself with friends and family. Their support carried him, and their shared disbelief and disgust at what I was doing brought him some comfort.

Meanwhile, my life continued to unravel. I began going to therapy every week. Most of my friends didn't know how to be a friend to someone they no longer understood, so my circle of friends dwindled to a select few. It soon became abundantly clear that I was, indeed, adrift at sea, all by myself.

Three weeks after I moved out, I was almost completely unhinged. My therapist instructed me to begin keeping a journal so I could unleash some of the anger and frustration that was eating me alive.

On November 20, I made a list of all the things I was upset about:

- Our plans to spend as much time together are falling apart.
- I don't know when I will see Ryan again.
- The startup has taken over Ryan's life completely, and I was not prepared for that.
- I feel left out.
- Our joint bank account is still empty, and I feel financially vulnerable.
- Abby's birthday is coming up, and the thought of Ryan spending any time with her hurts. A lot.
- No idea how the table setting/disengagement is going.
- No idea how the other legal stuff on Ryan's end is going.
- Not having a timeline or roadmap in place is really hard.

- Not know how we will manage a Denver/DC relationship. The distance and kids will make this tricky.

My life was a hot mess.

The nonstop texting and video chats dwindled in number. When Ryan and I did talk, it was no longer fun. Our conversations were awash in desperation – my desperation. For months, Ryan had been "setting the table" for Abby. It was his way of making it slowly but abundantly clear that he was exiting their marriage for me. He wanted to make things so unpleasant for her that she would break things off with him. The plan was that she would leave him. She would be so upset and so exhausted that she would end the marriage. Only then would he be free. Only then would we be together. I began peppering him with questions. "Is the table set yet? What has she been saying about me? What do you think is going through her mind? WHEN WILL SHE LEAVE YOU?" Instead of answers, I got lectures. He became less sympathetic. He had less patience and almost no time for me.

The long love letters also stopped arriving via email each morning. I used to read over and over how much he loved me and all the beautiful thoughts he had about our life together. And that was gone. I didn't want to get out of bed anymore. I did anyway, and then I'd stagger through my day, hoping time would fly.

Right after Thanksgiving, we had a long talk. Ryan was about to snap under the pressure of the startup and me.

"We really need to slow things down, Monika," he finally told me. "If we don't, our relationship will self-destruct. This is a bitter pill to swallow, but we have to – we both have to. I swear I am still setting the table for Abby every single day. In small ways and big ways. I still love you with all my being, but I also love Abby, and I love the kids, and I love my life. This is hard for me, too. I know you're struggling, but I am, too!"

Hold on. Back up. He loves Abby, the kids and his life. He loves Abby. He loves the kids. He loves his life. Could the red flag be bigger? Redder? More in-my-face than that?

Reality was trying to tell me something: "The party's over, Monika. Wake the fuck up. You are sitting in a goddamned beach chair, floating in the middle of the ocean, and you are all alone. No one is here, no one can see you, no one can save you. You have been abandoned out here. Sorry."

I never thought I'd be happy again. Happiness was something other people had but not me.

During the first weekend in December, I went holiday shopping with a new friend. Kate lived in the same apartment complex as me. She had two children, the same ages as mine, and she was separated from her husband. She was also the one who had moved out, and she also had a boyfriend – with whom she had spent a long weekend with in Vail. We were also on the same custody schedule, so we both had our kids during the same weeks. We bonded instantly.

As we shopped that Saturday, she randomly texted back and forth with Dan, her boyfriend. He always replied instantly. I texted Ryan when it began to snow. A couple of hours later, he texted back. "Nice – enjoy the snow! And have fun with Kate!" By then, the snow had ended, and I was back home, alone.

During the two months between my flight home from Denver and Christmas, more red flags appeared. I told you there'd be more, didn't I? Well, hold onto your hats, because you're in for some whoppers.

One day, we were talking on the phone when there was a knock at Ryan's door. "That's weird," he said. "Let me go see who's there. I'll call you right back."

He called me back about 15 minutes later, shaking and upset. Two FBI agents had showed up at his house with questions about an investment he was involved with years ago. He had told me about it over the summer – something to do with real estate. Well, now they wanted to talk to him – at their office in downtown Denver.

Meanwhile, we were arguing about money. He kept promising to send money to repay me for our New York and Chicago trips. I had paid for those very expensive hotels. I had picked up our shopping tabs. I had paid for food and that rental car in Denver. Combined with all the furniture I had purchased for my apartment – our apartment – all of which he had helped pick out and encouraged me to buy – I was $14,000 in the hole. On a nearly daily basis, he said he'd send me the money. I was growing increasingly frantic. Debt is not something I had ever lived with, and I wasn't going to start now. I did not need one more thing weighing me down.

Then one night, he didn't text me back. Even though we weren't in constant contact anymore, he never failed to text me back. "Now what?" I thought.

The next day, he called me as I was driving to therapy. I remember it so clearly. I had just gotten off the phone with my divorce attorney, and I was driving down a winding, tree-lined road. The sun was out, and the sky was blue. I was feeling somewhat stable, like I was finally finding my footing. But Ryan was acting odd, as if he was disconnected from me, from us. It was unsettling. He was barely paying attention to anything I said. Once I was fed up with repeating myself, I asked, "What on Earth is wrong with you? Is everything OK?"

"Yeah, everything's fine," he said. "So, you know my friend Scott?"

"Yup, you told me about him." Scott was a skateboarding buddy of Ryan's. He was divorced, but I didn't know much else about him. "He called me up yesterday and invited me out to a bar, just to hang out. I needed to blow off steam and get out of the house and away from work."

"You know what?" I replied. "That's a great idea. You do need to get out and spend time with friends. I'm glad you went."

"Yeah, me too," he said.

"You're lucky you're so distracted and busy!" I said. "I'm not. I wish I was, but I'm not."

"Well, why don't you go out and date? Have a fling!"

What the fuck?! If I did that, that would mean we were over. I don't want to fool around with someone else. I want to be with someone else – and I was talking to him on the phone right now!

To comfort myself, I focused on work and the kids. I drank a lot of wine and vodka. I read and went for walks. I tried to distract myself so I could make it through the holidays, and that meant pushing reality away. All I wanted to do was sleep. I wanted to go to sleep for a very long time and have someone wake me up when it was over.

Thanksgiving had been somewhat manageable, because friends took me in, but I still spent most of the long weekend all by myself. I had never felt so lonely in my life. Everyone was with family and friends, and for three long days, I was by myself. When you're bordering on the precipice of depression, being alone is not a good idea. The second hand on the clock ticked forward ever so slowly. E. and the kids spent the long holiday weekend with his family in New York, and they had a blast.

Now Christmas was looming. My parents and brothers were coming, and I was dreading it. I was not cheery or joyful or anything resembling merry. I was a sad wreck who was trying to prepare for three days of family time. My family loved me to death, but they were distraught about what was happening to me and my marriage and my kids. They were still very close to E. and talked to him often.

My family always stayed with us when they visited. Now I was living in a small two-bedroom apartment, and I had no place to put them. Luckily, a friend – one of the few I had left – loaned me her family's expansive house while they were away during Christmas break. This was a huge burden off my shoulders. My family had a comfortable place to sleep, and I had would get a break from them each night.

Despite my apprehension about having my family around, they were exceedingly gentle and kind. We were a rather loud bunch that laughed and teased each other constantly, but this time, everyone was subdued. No one poked me or harangued me – they were just there for me. They arrived wearing kid gloves, and I was cradled in their collective embrace.

On December 23, Ryan called me unexpectedly. He was at traffic court in Boulder, and though he wasn't happy to be there, he sounded like himself – happy and filled with love for his little pixie. We had a short but sweet conversation. My heart felt full once again, and a faint smile returned to my face.

On Christmas morning, as everyone dug into their Christmas stockings, I sat curled in the corner of my couch, by myself. I was drained. I couldn't keep up the fake good cheer anymore. My dad noticed and said, "Monika, why don't you come sit over here with us?" His face was filled with love and concern for me.

"No, I'm fine," I responded in a very small voice. I sunk deeper in the cushions, trying to disappear. But then things weren't fine.

At 5:03pm on Christmas Day, I emailed Ryan through tears.

Hi baby,

I hope you are having a much better Xmas than me. I just left my place - and I don't want to go back. I am sitting in my car in a parking lot.

My entire family is indeed going to E.'s tomorrow. They are on his side, not mine - my dad said so. My mom was sitting right there - and did not contradict him. And then he starts hammering away at me about how it was a huge mistake to leave E., etc. And so I just ignored him, waiting for him to stop. But he didn't stop - he kept going and going so finally I exploded at him and with a merry FUCK YOU I grabbed my coat, shoes, purse and keys and left - in tears.

My brother just called saying my dad wanted to talk, but I refused. I said he had to leave. This is the worst Xmas ever, compounded by the fact that I hardly slept last night.

I love you Ryan - and I have never missed you more than I do right now.

XOXO,
M

The next night, Ryan wrote back.

I have been trying for hours to decide how to respond to your email ... and waiting to have the time to respond with everyone still home.

I've arrived at this: 1) I think your family is right and 2) Enough is enough.

Your ordeal last night sounds awful, and I'm so very, very sorry you had to go through it. Your family is obviously set on not listening to your reasons for not wanting to be with E. ... or perhaps they just don't believe you. Or maybe they see something that I don't ... or something you can't - or know something that I don't ... know something about you, about your life with E. ... the kids - I just don't know. This much is obvious: their position is not wavering, and maybe it's time to investigate why ... maybe it's time to stop fighting them and listen to what they have to say. Maybe in this case they are right? Here's why I think maybe they are: They know you better than anyone. They care for you more than anyone. They have only your best interests at heart, not their own. They are your parents, and they are devastated ... why?? I simply don't know... and that's really what keeps nagging me - I simply don't know. I don't know them, I don't know you, I don't know E. ... I don't really know anything.

And that is the root of the problem - I don't know you ... don't know anything about you really, and that's the truth.

Once again, this situation is harkening back to the main problem with our relationship: from day one, everything went too fast, and now the bill's come due. You need no more proof than to look at how you signed your email last night – using my last name. You started doing that in, what - August?? - just 4 months ago!?? In a matter of days, you decided that you wanted to spend the rest of your life with me ... that was simply crazy, was crazy then, it's crazy now - everything has been too crazy, too fast, too scary - for everyone, including us. We have acted like lunatics escaped from the asylum ... we've behaved irrationally and atrociously. We constructed this fantasy world in which everything we did was logical, sensible and rational. We imagined this "mountain" that we had to climb to get our way, and expected everyone around us to believe us to be right. In fact, we have been dead wrong from the start - you know it, I know it ... and enough is enough.

Here's one thing I DO know for sure. Your family despises me, and everything I stand for. Nothing will ever change that. Nothing. Ever. And you know what? I DON'T BLAME THEM! Not one bit, and I would feel the same way if I were them. Monika, maybe there's some truth in their position. Maybe you should listen to them...I know you wanted a change from E., but in all honesty, that's ALL I KNOW! I know nothing of your past but what you've told me ... I don't know E., I never saw him in "action" being the person you describe ... so I can't speak to the truth of anything.

And here's something else I DO know: I'm losing faith in what little I do know about you and your past with E.

And here's what else I know: despite what I begged and pleaded of you, you left E. for me ... I told you then I couldn't live with that burden no matter what the future held, and that still stands ... more now than ever. I will not be a home wrecker ... I won't carry that label with me. It was wrong - a huge mistake - and it needs to be rectified starting now. I should never have let myself fill the void left by that other guy ... I knew it was happening, you knew it was happening, yet we both the did the EXACT wrong thing, and did nothing to stop it. Very, very stupid. Very, very selfish. Very, very wrong. I should have done more to stop you, I know this, and will always feel a tremendous amount of guilt for that. But that's spilt milk - and enough is enough.

I have no idea if you belong with E. or not ... and frankly, I don't know if YOU know it or not. But your family believes that you owe it to them ... and to your children to find out for sure. It has to be a decision on its own merits, not because I - or anyone else - is part of the picture. You need to figure out if you want to be married to E., period. Not whether you'd rather be with me or anybody else for that matter ... or whether you'd like some change in your life, or some variety, or some peace, or ... whatever! You need to decide on your own, without me or anybody else in the wings, if he's the right person for you. Despite everything that's happened, I honestly believe at this point that you still haven't made that decision. Your decision was that you wanted to be with me more than him, and though I begged you to make your decisions based on what was right for you, you and I both know you didn't. And that simply isn't right - and simply isn't fair to you, your kids, your family - even E. ... and I's DEFINITELY not something that will stand the test of time. And enough is enough.

So I am doing the right thing, and removing myself from the picture before it's too late. We need to stop. Deep down, you know it's the right thing ... maybe not now, but eventually you will. You need to realize something very, very important right now: I am not worth it - WE are not worth it - not worth this pain, this destruction and heartache. I don't know if any man or woman is, but I know that I certainly am not - that's not self-deprecating, that's truth, plain and simple.

And here's what ELSE I know: I can't go on like this - I simply have too much on my own plate to worry about yours ... and can no longer carry the burden of the unbearable sadness for which I am now solely to blame in your life. With my health issues, my possible legal issues, the new company - and everything else - I simply don't have the luxury - nor the intention - of making ANY decisions about my future anytime soon ... I am simply trying to deal with the present, and that's proving hard enough.

When we first met, all you did was rave about your family, and I have torn that asunder. It's time to make amends. I will shoulder the blame for my part, but you must shoulder yours ... we both made too many mistakes to count ... both made promises we couldn't keep - wrote checks we could never cash. It's time to stop ... time to step back, look at the mess, and begin to clean it up. You need your family, Monika - everybody does - this distance and heartache between you and them can't continue. As long as I am part of the picture, there's no chance that any healing is going to take place between you and them. And I mean NEVER ... and I simply can't live with that. So I am removing myself from the picture.

I am sorry it has to be this way, but it does, and you know it. Now is simply not our time, it just isn't.

If you want to hate me, hate me. If you want to blame me, blame me. If you want to be furious with me, be furious with me. If you want to tell everyone that I ruined everything, then tell them. All I care about is your happiness, your children's happiness, and your relationship with your family getting back to where it was before we met. None of this is possible with me involved with your life. I am to blame for so much sadness and hurt in your life - ALL OF IT IN FACT - and I simply can't go on adding to this mess - I just cannot. It's high time that I take the first step and start being part of the solution and not part of the problem. As deeply heart breaking as this is for me -and obviously you as well – it's the right thing to do, now, before any further permanent destruction and decisions have been made. Enough is enough.

We can talk about this as much as you want on Wednesday. Abby will be back to work and the kids will be gone, so we can vid. Until then, please just try to give all of this the careful thought it deserves. Once the sadness begins to part, you will see the truth in it - this is the right thing to do for everyone, and I do mean EVERYONE, involved. We've thought selfishly only of ourselves, made crazy, stupid decisions, frightened our loved ones, caused pain and heartache, and now we have to pay that bill. I know you will find fault with much I have written here at first, but I hope upon further reflection, you will come to the realization that I am simply laying out facts.

It's really that simple. We're not kids, Monika, we're adults, we have responsibilities to others, friends and family alike. We just don't have the right to continue on - there are too many people whose lives our relationship has impacted negatively ... much to our shame and regret I fear. But it's never too late. Nothing has been done that can't be undone. We can plead the insanity of "young love", forgive ourselves for our mistakes, and move forward and make life wonderful for ourselves and the people we care about ... that's all we can do as humans, ultimately.

I will always love you, Monika.

R.

I responded immediately.

I literally cannot believe what you wrote to me Ryan. Literally.

You found me. You came after me. You worked your darndest to turn me around and look at you. And I did.

And now you are throwing us away. Just chucking me by the wayside. You were the one who said you'd leave Abby for me. You were the one who started talking marriage, when all I was thinking was, wow, this guy is something else and I want to get to know him - he is so fucking cool. You said I was the love of your life and you'd never let me go - not once, but multiple times. Now, when it's hard, when I am having a tough time, when you are having a tough time, you just throw up your hands and call it quits. That is not fair - and that is the meanest thing anyone has ever done to me.

You did not come between me and my family. They just don't know why I left a seemingly perfect person who they were not married to. I don't know why, but my dad does not want to accept it, while my brothers and my mom are trying to. And I don't know how many times I told you, but I did NOT leave E. for you for chrissakes. I left him for me. I am starting to wonder if anyone listens to me. And for fuck's sake my family does not despise you. I told you multiple times how difficult my father can be - and yes, they just want me to be happy - and I am or was or whatever. I don't even know right now.

And now you are saying you don't believe in me or believe me. That hurts. Because I both believe in you and believe you. I am just bowled over that you said you don't know anything about me - really?! I thought we did slow things down, and I was trying to be patient, to be like, OK, this is temporary. But now you can't even be bothered.

I am crushed, literally crushed. I knew none of this would be easy, but now you've just crushed me. I can't even really collect my thoughts because I am shocked beyond belief. You, of all people - I completely and totally trusted you unlike anyone else - and this is what you do to me? To us? How the fuck can you do that? How can you do this to me? To just run away?

I don't want us to end, and I don't want to let you go. No one has ever made me as happy as you have in the few months I have known you. I accepted all of the obstacles in the way of us, and I started in anyway. And you did too, with eyes fully open. Life has gotten in the way - and that is what happens sometimes. But I honestly cannot believe you want us to end. Yes, we went in too fast - like idiotic teenagers. All I am trying to do is be there for you, to help you with everything, from work to health stuff, and you are pushing me away like I don't matter - like I was just a fun something but oh well, life sucks, too bad, deal with it Monika. I had been signing my name with your last initial because I THOUGHT you had every intention of leaving Abby for me because that is what you always said - and you always said the end of the year, and I said fine, the end of the year. And you are reneging on everything. I feel like I am in a very bad dream, I really do.

We are going to have to find a lot of time to talk about this, because Ryan, I am NOT letting you go. I believe in us. And I hope you still do too.

***

The next morning, I was in a haze. My family brought the kids to E.'s house and celebrated a second Christmas with him and his parents. I surveyed my empty apartment, slowly picked things up and put my sad life back together. I moved the kids' gifts into their room, did laundry, packed away Christmas cookies, and gazed at the Christmas tree, hoping it would bring me some comfort.

That night, I received an email from Ryan and watched the last few cards flutter to the floor.

I understand your anger, I understand your sadness, I understand your need to blame me - and I understand your need to "hit" me with all that. I also understand that it will take some time for this phase to pass, and for you to really listen to what I'm saying before you're going to see the truth in it. Once that happens, I hope you will begin to see that, once again, I am simply laying out facts as they are, not trying to present a bunch of topics for discussion in the vein of "he said/she said"... that's not my intention, nor my desire. I understand your need to over simplify the situation and be accusatory ... I am simply trying to move forward in the most positive way possible.

*And yes, they are very painful facts, but they are what they are ... and **we** have gone about this all wrong from the beginning, plain and simple. Unfortunately, it can't simply be brushed off by saying "Yes, we went in too fast - like idiotic teenagers." **We've** caused people pain, **we've** caused people heartache, **we've** caused people to doubt our sanity ... mostly though **we've** just been wrong - everything has been wrong from the start. This is just fact - I'm not trying to start a discussion about it, because that's pointless ... it just is what it is.*

*I understand that you are hurt by the things I've said ... they hurt me too ... but the reason they hurt is because they are true. You can say what you want, but the fact of the matter remains, yes, I do honestly believe **we** don't know each other ... EVERYONE ELSE can see that plain as day, it's time we did as well. Even if we lived in the same city, and dated EVERY day for 4 months,* people would still be suspicious of our relationship, and rightly so ... can't you see that? Even four months of seeing each other every single day is STILL NOTHING from any rational perspective. And we have WAY LESS than that! That's just fact. Any true friend who came to you and said "hey, I met this great guy, we've dated for four months, and we're going to get married" you would view with suspicion, and you should. You would say "4 months??!! You don't even know the guy!" And that would be true - and that's everyone else's response to us. Once again Monika, it's not everyone else is wrong, and we are right. **We** are wrong, period.

I have ABSOLUTELY come between you and your family, and in a very sinister way...especially from their point of view. I'm not going to debate this, it's a fact. And they are right. Likewise, your children and your friends ... everything in your personal life has come completely undone since I entered the picture ... I have been a force of destruction, and I can't live with it any longer.

To categorize my decision as "running away" I think is very short-sighted. In fact, I would argue, I'm the only one of us that's confronting this mess head-on. We cannot continue as is...we simply can't. To ignore that reality ... to ignore the damage being done all around us, THAT is running away ... THAT is cowardly in my opinion. I am doing the right thing, and I know it. I know it is painful, but that's the bill **we** cooked up for ourselves.

I would also argue that neither of us had "eyes fully open" ... it's naive to think that, and immature. **We've** had blinders on from the very beginning, and ignored every bit of common sense between us ... but that's what "love" does, it blinds people ... so what, we're human. However, that realization does not absolve **us** from doing what's right at this point.

And if you need to bottle it up and package it as me "reneging on everything", then so be it. I don't think it's fair, but if it makes you feel better then go ahead. You know very well I don't think it was "just a fun something", and I know once your anger begins to subside, you will know that's not a fair statement. Likewise, to say I'm "chucking it by the wayside" is a ridiculous statement - I'm in as much pain as you right now, and you know it. But it's what we have to endure so that we can take the pain away from those around us ... your family, your kids, your friends - they deserve better, and since I came into your life, all those people have been chucked by the wayside. Enough is enough.

*It's no longer a matter of believing in us, Monika ... I don't know what "us" even is because everything from the start has been so completely ass-backwards ... so irrational, so wrong-headed. I'm not happy being the one who has to do this, but one of us had to, and you know it. There are simply too many other lives to consider, **we're** adults, and **we** must start acting that way. **We** simply don't have the right to continue ignoring those around us.*

I hope you will share what I've written with your parents, your brothers, your therapist ... and anyone else you want. I am absolutely 100% sure that they would see the truth in what I am saying, and would be happy to tell you it's the right thing to do ... especially your family. And they are the only people who matter - crazy as they are, they are truly the only people who matter ... but you already know that. It may take you some time to acknowledge it, but you already know it.

I'm happy to consider pushing the reset button, and going back to basics like, "hi, I'm me, nice to meet you" and actually getting to know each other for a while ... but I won't consider continuing on with what "we" are now. No more talk of marriage, no more talk of your divorce and its proceedings, no more talk about our future life together, no more talk about moving here and there ... you have too much on your plate that you need to deal with and sort out without promises from me (or anyone else) to distort your perspective. You are making life changing decisions ... your life, your kid's lives, your family's ... your friend's ... these are WAY too important to be clouded by "what if's" regarding me or anyone else. I cannot be a part of your process any longer, it's not fair to anyone, least of all you.

*And my focus is going to be primarily on this company I'm building and the rest of my work. I have let it suffer IMMEASURABLY over the last 4 months, and that will not continue. No more daily vids, no more spending an hour writing you an email ... none of it. We have both let our priorities become completely screwed up, and I will not continue on this path for both of our sakes. That's the only "us" I will consider, other than that, my life and my future are way too uncertain to allow anything else. It was all too easy for **us** to just throw all these considerations by the wayside in **our** greedy desire to create a fantasy world to live in, all too easy to just take the complexity of our separate realities and completely ignore it...hoping blindly that it would just go away.*

73

I will accept my responsibility for my reckless behavior, and for foolish things said that shouldn't have been said over the course of our relationship, I am only human, and I know I have made my fair share of mistakes along the way, and will shoulder that for a long time to come. But I will not shoulder it alone, and if that's what you expect, then we have nothing to talk about.

P.S - I know you think it's crazy that Abby has proposed an open relationship, but as I have talked more about it with her, I understand why an open relationship is not only important, but vital to a happy and fulfilling married relationship - and I think it's probably one of the most interesting and invigorating changes I've ever been through, now that I've accepted and understand it.

All I know from you is that you think it's crazy. So I ask you - would you ever consider this arrangement? Would you be able to allow me to pursue my desires and take some chick back to her place for a one night stand, when and if the urge to do so arose? And if you think that I'm not that person, not interested or inclined towards that sort of behavior, then you don't know me, because I am that person. And if it's not something you would consider, then you should know that I'm not inclined to give up what I have been given in the last couple months for going back to more of the same.

This is part of who I am, and if you knew me, you'd already know this. I have no idea your response to this, again, because I don't know you. I don't know if maybe you'd want to go and do the same ... go pick up some guy just to fuck him ... I would be fine with it, but I have no idea if that's something you'd do ... we just don't know each other.

Chapter 4

Wake Up

I was in shock, completely stripped to the core. I was no longer floating out in the ocean by myself. I had now been marooned on an island and transformed into bone-dry, rusty old bucket in the desert.

I didn't know it would take three months before I started feeling like myself. All I knew was this: I was gutted.

After re-reading Ryan's email, gasping and sobbing through every wrenching sentence, I called one of my closest friends. Meg had stood by me no matter what – the mark of a true friend. She dropped everything and rushed to my apartment, bringing along the makings for BLTs. According to Meg, BLTs fix everything.

Needless to say, Meg was outraged after she read the email. You could probably hear her ranting and raving from miles away. Her summation of what Ryan had done: "He's an immature coward. He got what he wanted, and then walked away, leaving scorched earth behind him."

She stayed with me for a few hours, but eventually, she had to get home to her own family and her own life.

As I sat alone in my dark apartment, I realized how utterly spent I was. I was too exhausted to be angry. I had given all of me – my love, energy, attention, hope and happiness – to someone who never deserved it. Ryan had gobbled up every bit of me, and now I was left with nothing.

I slept for 10 hours.

The next morning, I couldn't even get out of bed. I stared at the ceiling. I turned on my side and blinked at the stitching on my duvet cover. I willed myself back to sleep.

My ringing phone woke me up. I picked it up and saw the caller ID. It was my dad.

"Hello?" I whispered.

"Hi Monika, it's your dad."

"Yeah, I know," I replied weakly.

Hearing the defeat in my voice, he immediately said, "What's wrong? Are you OK?"

And then it all spilled out. The email. The devastation. The emptiness.

"Honey, why don't you come home for a few days. The kids are with E. Come home and spend time with me and your mom."

As a parent, there is nothing worse than knowing your child is hurting. All you want to do is help. I was so damaged that nothing could really be done for me, beyond offering a warm embrace.

I packed up a few days' worth of clothes and drove five hours in the waning winter sun to my hometown in New York. When I was almost home, I called E.

"Hello?" he answered warily. I could hear laughter in the background.

"Hi. How are the kids?"

"Good! My parents are here, and we're just about to eat dinner."

"Great." I cleared me throat. "Um, so I got an email from Ryan. He basically dumped me, so, yeah, I wanted you to know that. And, um, also, I'm really sorry for everything, E. I'm so sorry."

"Thanks," he said. After a moment of silence – of registering what I just said – he asked, "Do you want to talk to the kids?"

I chatted with them briefly. They were distracted, as they were busy playing with their new toys. I told them I was driving up to New York to visit their grandparents and that I'd talk to them tomorrow.

After everything I had put my parents through, they were thrilled to have me home. We didn't do much – played cards, read in front of a roaring fire, went for walks. It was perfect. It was just what I needed. They gave me my space, but were always right there if I needed them.

One night, they took me to a favorite restaurant for dinner – a white tablecloth restaurant that serves exquisite Italian food. Everything is made in-house, the service is outstanding, the lights are dim, and ambience is hushed. The last time I had dined there, it had been with E. when I was four months pregnant with our daughter. A lifetime ago.

After we ordered, my dad asked the inevitable question: "Why don't you try to work things out with E.?"

I looked across the table at my mom. She avoided my eyes and continued to look at my dad.

"It's complicated, Dad. I don't know."

And I didn't. I didn't know. I didn't know what I wanted or who I was or where I was going. I needed a lot of time to sort myself out.

The next morning, I drove down to the Bronx to visit my best friend, Annie. We had been inseparable since the day she and her family moved into the house next door to my parent's. It was one of those perfect sunny days right after a huge snowstorm. They pulled up to the house, followed closely behind by a moving van, as we shoveled our driveway. It was 1983, and we have been the best of friends ever since.

Annie and I talked and talked. She listened sympathetically to my sad tale of woe as had brunch at a local Irish bar and wandered around the Bronx Zoo. Annie updated me on her life – her job, her husband and kids, her parents. It was nice to focus on someone else's normal, uncomplicated life for a little while.

The next day, I drove home and slowly began putting my life back together.

Work was no longer the solace it had been. I completed my tasks with zero joy. I was just going through the motions. I didn't have much energy to attend networking events and seek out new clients, so my work load lightened. On one hand, this was good – I needed the mental break. But on the other hand, my bank account grew smaller and smaller.

I know you're wondering if I was still working with Ryan. The answer: yes. We both still worked for the media company. I was still Editor, and he was still the graphic designer. The good thing about being emotionally gutted is that you don't really care. I didn't care that I still had to communicate with him, but I did keep it to the very bare minimum. I may have been curt or even rude, but too bad. I didn't owe him anything.

Can you believe that he continued to flirt with me? He continued to write, "As you wish" when I asked him for something. Asshole.

During the weeks I had the kids, I was very focused on them and doing as many fun things as I could manage. We went to the movies, I took them to birthday parties, we played board games and did crafts. On Saturday mornings, I took them to swim lessons at the local Y. On Sunday mornings, we went to my son's indoor soccer league, where he worked on his skills with other 5- and 6-year olds.

During the weeks I was alone, I read, watched TV and continued to drink a lot of wine and vodka. I got together with friends, but not very often. It was too much work.

One of the brightest moments in my life came each Wednesday at 11am when I had my weekly therapy appointment. I lived for these sessions. I worked on understanding my behavior, forgiving myself, being kinder and gentler to myself and others. If I had learned anything over the past year, it was that I needed to change. I was committed to learning from my mistakes and becoming a newer, better version of me.

Ever so slowly, I started feeling like myself. The empty rusty bucket I had become slowly filled with water. Some of it spilled and some of it evaporated, but it began to fill up once again.

During this time, I was able to see Ryan for who he really was: a sociopath and fully-fledged con artist who manipulated, took advantage of and then gaslighted me. He is a cruel and awful human being, rotten to the core. He easily laid so much blame on me. Yes, I played a part in our ridiculous affair. I completely own that. I'm not proud of it, but I have come to terms with it. Ryan, however, steered the ship and then tossed me overboard when I became inconvenient.

Let's talk about what a sociopath is. For me, it has always conjured an image of a serial killer in a B-rated horror movie – but after turning to Google, I realized that's a psychopath. A sociopath:

- Lacks empathy and can be cold, unfeeling, callous and overly critical
- Has no regard for boundaries, rules or laws
- Is charismatic and charming; they use humor, flattery, intellect, or flirtation for personal gain
- Is impulsive
- Is arrogant
- Is psychically or verbally abusive

Yup, that describes Ryan to a T. So does the definition of a con artist. Con artists are deceptive. They lie, cheat and fool people. They prey on weaknesses. They have no conscience.

If we review Ryan's behavior, it is obvious he embodies these horrible traits. He lied nonstop. He promised me the sun, the moon and the stars. And then he tried to gaslight me and lay all the blame at my feet. He preyed on me. He worked hard for months to get me to notice him. He convinced me to leave E. He then convinced me that E. was a useless idiot. He wrote us a fairytale life of wealth, health, travel and boundless happiness. He dragged me along, promising to leave Abby. And then the con was up. When the con fails, there's only one thing to do: Get out of there as fast as possible.

It was very hard for me to come to terms with who Ryan really was. I was very angry at him for his cruelty. I was angry at myself for falling for him. I was angry that I had trusted him so completely. I was angry that I had been so easily hoodwinked. Anger will eat you from the inside out, so I had to let it go. I couldn't change what had happened. I could only change what would happen next.

What happened next was my own Eat Pray Love vacation. If you didn't read the book, you saw the movie with Julia Roberts, so you know the story: Woman's life falls apart. She takes a break from her life and travels around the world, learning a lot about herself along the way and finally meeting the love of her life (who she is now divorced from, which just doesn't seem right, but that's beside the point).

I did not travel around the world, but I did go to Hawaii.

My brother had been living in Hawaii for around eight months, where he was working on his PhD. If you know anything about PhD programs, most take a few to several years to complete, and a faculty member must sponsor you, which is how he ended up at the University of Hawaii. Not a shabby place to live and study. And not a shabby place to go on vacation.

I had worked it out with E. He had the kids the week before spring break, and I had them the week of spring break. He would drive them to my parent's beach house in New Jersey the weekend spring break began. When I got home from Hawaii, I would meet my kids and parents in New Jersey.

As I began to pack, I realized I only needed a carry-on suitcase. I would spend most of the trip in my bathing suit, so I didn't need a ton of clothes. And I was staying with my brother in his crappy apartment in Waikiki Beach, so I didn't need any fancy clothes. The space in my suitcase not being taken up by clothes was filled with books by Michael Pollen (kind of heavy reading for the beach, but enjoyable nonetheless) and my journal.

When I landed in Honolulu, I had no idea I was about to take the most important vacation of my life. I was just excited to be in Hawaii and see my baby brother (he's 10 years younger than me and therefore will always be my baby brother). As I walked into the main terminal, I spotted my brother at once. "Welcome to Hawaii, Nonny" – that's his pet name for me – and then he wrapped me in a bear hug before placing a lei around my neck. We piled into his roommate's pickup truck and traversed the dark roads of Honolulu. Lights from various neighborhoods flickered up the side of an extinct volcano. Warm salty air whipped through the open windows. The sound of waves could be heard in the distance.

It was midweek – and mid-way through my brother's spring break. We had a few days together before he was back at school. The first day there, I instantly regretted packing only flip-flops to wear. Flip-flops are not walking shoes. They give you blisters, even if they're

Havianas. My brother and I walked past a golf course, sundry shops, a school, and the zoo until we reached the beach. He showed me his favorite spot, which was quiet and uncrowded. It immediately became my go-to beach. After sunning ourselves in the shade of a palm tree, reading, and swimming in the clear blue ocean, we walked down the beach towards Diamond Head and then turned and walked into the tourist mania that is Waikiki Beach. Vacationers marched into and out of oceanfront resorts, weaved up and down the sidewalks and searched for aloe vera to cool their sunburns. By the time we turned to walk home, I was barefoot, Havianas in hand. Despite the blisters, I was happy as a clam.

The next day, my brother's roommate was off work, so we drove up to the North Shore. We zoomed along the highway that connects sprawling Honolulu to the quiet towns on the North Shore, passing acres and acres of pineapple farms. We crested the hill and stared straight ahead towards the endless blue ocean. We spent the afternoon hopping from beach to beach. The boys surfed, and I sunned – mostly in the shade of palm trees. The next day, my brother and I ate our way through the Saturday farmer's market before retreating to our favorite beach. That night, we decided to go with his roommate to the west coast of Oahu, where his roommate would be lifeguarding.

The west coast – past the glamour and glitz of the big Disney resort – is rugged and lightly populated. The people who do live there are very poor. Violence, substance abuse and domestic abuse are common. We drove past an enormous homeless encampment that had been haphazardly arranged in the scrub between the road and the beach.

We dropped of his roommate, and my brother and I drove to the end of the road. We were as far west as we could get. The beach was a postcard: White sand, aqua sea, blue sky, bright sun. But no shade. After swimming with my brother for a while, I settled on my blanket and propped open my book. The words soon became a blurry mess. A headache started to form. I stood up to wave in my brother to shore and felt dizzy. He didn't see me. When his head bobbed to the surface again, I waved again, but still, he didn't see me. I began to panic. I looked around the beach. A few people were scattered here and there. About 20 feet away were two old men chatting away in the shade of their umbrella.

I walked towards them. "Excuse me!" I called.

They turned and looked at me. "Hello!" they replied.

"Hi. So, I am feeling really dizzy and my brother is in the water and doesn't see me waving at him. Could I possibly sit under your umbrella with you?"

"Oh yes, dear," one of them immediately responded. "Of course you can sit with us."

"Absolutely," the other said. "We have cold water. Do you need a bottle?"

"Yes, that would be great," I said. "I have a bottle, but the water isn't very cold anymore. Let me go get my towel. I'll be right back." And these two sweet retirees took care of me until my brother finally got out of the water.

When you are suffering from heat exhaustion, it is hard to drink enough water to fully recover. It took me a full day – and I drink a lot of water even when I'm not at the beach. Once my brother was done swimming, we piled into the pickup, blasted the A/C and drove off to find me some food, coconut water and shade. I've spent my life going to the beach, and I have never had heat exhaustion. A word to the wise: don't get it.

For the next few days, I was on my own. My brother went to school, my roommate went to work, and I went to Starbucks in the morning to check email and work a bit before heading to "my" beach. For most of the day, I was alone. But not only was I alone, I was away from the demands of "real" life. Having that space – that mental, emotional and physical space – was a gift. Of course, it didn't hurt that I was in Hawaii! But that space allowed for a lot of self-reflection. Who was I? What did I want? I had wiped my life clean and now I had this blank slate. What did I want to fill it with?

The languid days in Hawaii ensured I didn't rush my thoughts. They slowly filtered in and out of my mind, some hanging around, some flitting away. Finally, on my last day in Hawaii, my rusty old bucket was filled to the brim with fresh, clear water.

I knew what I wanted, and I knew what I needed to do next.

I wanted E. back. I wanted to rebuild my marriage, and I wanted to undo the tremendous damage I had so carelessly strewn all around me.

I knew it was not going to be easy, but the gravity of what I had done and the long road in front of me didn't full come into focus until I was back at the airport, waiting for my flight home. I called my mom, panicked and nearly hysterical.

"Hi Mom," my voice quavered and then the tears and words rushed out in a torrent. "I'm at the airport and my flight is delayed and I had to check my carry-on back, which is stupid because it's a carry-on bag – there's a reason I only brought a carry-on – and so I'm standing here waiting for my flight and all I can think about is what I have done – what a mess I made over the past several months and I want to fix my marriage and fix my life and I don't know if it'll work and I'm really scared. I'm scared, Mom."

People were staring at me. It's not unusual to see someone crying at an airport, but this wasn't crying. This was heaving desperation.

"Oh honey." The sadness and pity in my mom's voice were almost too much for me to bear. I could tell she just wanted to hug me. I've never needed a hug more in my life than at that moment. I needed someone to hold me and comfort me and tell me it was going to be OK. But she couldn't do that. No one could.

"Do you think E. will take me back, Mom?"

"I don't know, I really don't. But you can start by talking to him."

84

"I will, Mom." I sighed. "I really messed up. I can't believe what I did, and I'm so sorry."

"I know you are, honey."

We talked a little longer. My mom tried to comfort me and I tried to be comforted.

During the first leg of my flight, which took us to San Francisco, I thought. What would I say to E.? How would he react? What will it take for us to get back together? Would he even entertain the idea? What would happen if he took me back? What will our lives look like, what will our marriage be like? What happens if he doesn't take me back? Then what?

No. I told myself I was not going to fail. I had already done plenty of failing in the past 11 months. No more failing.

I tried to sleep on the flight from San Francisco to DC, but my mind would not shut down. "What if…?" played over and over in my head.

Soon enough, we were approaching Washington Dulles International Airport. It was cold and sunny, but that sunshine gave me hope.

I was not going to fail.

Chapter 5

Rebuilding

As soon as the red-eye landed, I texted E.

"I'd like to talk to you. Can I come over?"

"Sure," he replied.

I scurried off the plane and through the airport. Once I got outside the main terminal, I practically ran to my car. Adrenaline beat back the exhaustion as I turned the key in the ignition and pulled out of the parking garage. Our house is only 10 minutes from the airport, and as I got closer, I got more and more nervous. By the time I pulled into the driveway, I was almost hyperventilating.

I knocked on the door. E. opened it, and I said, "Hi. Can I come in?"

"Yes."

He stood back, and I walked into his – our – house. He walked past me and into the kitchen, where he was making coffee. I sat on a bar stool in the breakfast area.

I cleared my throat. E. looked at me expectantly. "So, I did a lot of thinking while I was in Hawaii, and I understand the gravity of what I did. I destroyed our marriage, and I destroyed our lives. I was manipulated by Ryan, who saw that I was vulnerable and took full advantage of it. I let him whisk me away to a new life, when all he was doing was lying and making promises he couldn't and didn't want to keep. I'm so, so sorry for what I did. I've been working really hard in therapy, and I understand what I did and why I did it. I've worked hard to make changes, to raise my awareness about how I react in certain situations, and basically to be a better Monika. A newer, better Monika. I would like to try to rebuild our marriage. I don't want to be separated anymore. I don't want to divorce. I want to get back together. I realized I never stopped loving you and that I still love you very much."

"Wow," E. said. "Um, thank you for your apology. I appreciate it."

I smiled.

"But," he continued as my smile disappeared, "you can't just Ryanz in here and expect everything to be OK. You really hurt me, Monika. I was devastated. Devastated! I lost almost 30 lbs. I couldn't eat, I couldn't sleep, I could barely function at work. You put me through hell. You put the kids through hell. And I can't forget that."

I choked back tears. "I know, I know what I did! I am very aware of what I did! I'm asking you to please give me a second chance. Please!"

"That's something I have to think about," E. said. "But right now, I need to focus on finding a new job. I am getting laid off, and I need to focus on keeping a roof over my head."

"Oh my god!" I said. "I'm so sorry! Is there anything I can do?"

"No," E. shook his head. "I just need space to think about what you said and to hunt for a job. That's my priority right now. It might not be yours, but it's in your best interest for me to get a new job."

"Right, I understand," I said.

"But if I'm even going to consider it, you need to answer a question," E. said. "Do not lie. You need to tell me the truth."

"OK."

"Did you have an affair with Will?"

My jaw dropped open. How did he know? How did he know about my first affair?

"Um."

"Monika, don't lie."

"No, I didn't! I swear!"

I was panicked. Even though he knew, I was too ashamed to admit it. I had done enough damage with Ryan. I didn't want to talk about Will. No! No Will! Just lie and move on.

"Are you sure? You didn't have an affair last summer with Will?"

"No."

"OK, fine. I think it's time for you to go."

"OK," I muttered as I slid off the bar stool. "I better go home, unpack, repack and head to the beach to see the kids."

"Yeah, sounds good."

E. walked me to the door, and shut it softly behind me.

89

I don't know how I stayed awake on the 3 ½ hour drive to the beach house, but I did. The kids were beyond excited to see me. I hugged them hello, listened to their happy chatter for a while, and then trudged upstairs to my room for a nap.

It was a miserable Easter weekend for me. I knew that E. was seeing someone, but I didn't know that they were planning a getaway over Easter weekend to a romantic inn in Charlottesville. I didn't know, until I called him while he was driving in the car with her.

I had called to see if he could talk to the kids. "I'm in the car, so I can't talk right now," he said.

"Sure you can," I insisted. "You can talk while you drive. You do it all the time."

"No, Monika," E. said firmly. "I'm in the car with Stacy, so I can't talk to the kids right now."

"Where are you going?" I demanded.

"We're headed to dinner in Charlottesville."

"That's a long drive for dinner." Charlottesville is 2 ½ hours from where we live.

"No, we're here for the weekend."

That simple sentence landed like a punch to the gut – the gut that I had been working hard to fill back up with love and laughter and positivity and the new, better Monika.

I quickly hung up. And then I was hysterical the rest of the weekend. Yes, I realize this is hypocritical of me. E. was trying to move on. He deserved to have fun and companionship and sex. I had only just sprung on him the fact that I wanted to get back together. That's a lot to process – I understood that intellectually. But though he may have deserved happiness and a long weekend away with someone he liked, I was devastated. The bruises and batters on my heart that were nearly healed turned purple all over again.

I was also extremely angry with myself. My therapist, mom, aunt and a few friends all said the same thing: I had to forgive myself. Yes, I made a big mistake, but I'm human and was sorry for my mistake. "Stop beating yourself up!" they'd say.

Once the kids and I returned home in Virginia, the real work began. Each day moved ever so slowly. I just wanted answers. Would E. take me back? Could we make this work? Did he want to put our marriage back together?

Living in that kind of limbo took its toll on me. Despite all the work I put into healing, I was still very fragile. There was a lot of crying and a lot of phone calls. If I could get even a tiny bit of reassurance from someone, I grabbed it. I called my parents constantly. I called my brothers and best friend. I called my aunt and uncles. I called the friends who had stuck by me. I called the minister who had married us and who I had known for decades.

Hearing words of sympathy, reassurance and love became my new addiction. That, and vodka. I drank a lot of it, chugging it straight from the bottle so I could sleep at night.

Whenever I talked to E., I tried to convince him to take me back, to go to therapy, to give me a second chance. "I have changed!" I always reminded him. "I have changed so much, but you won't see those changes until we start spending time together."

I had to go through what I put him through. It was a condensed and less sinister and malicious version of what I put him through, but it still hurt.

In fact, it hurt a lot. No amount of crying, vodka, talking, journal-writing or therapy could help. I called my doctor on a Thursday in late April and made an emergency appointment for later that day. I was desperate, and I needed help.

Dr. G walked into the exam room to find me curled up in a fetal position, sobbing. I explained what was happening through sobs. She nodded slowly and listened carefully. When I was done talking, so asked me some questions. No, I was not suicidal. No, I didn't want to hurt anyone. My answers satisfied her, and she wrote me a prescription for anti-depressants.

I was not prepared for the speed at which the anti-depressants would kick in. For the first week, I slept a lot. I already sleep a lot – 9 hours a night, on average – but now I was sleeping for 11 or 12 hours. When I finally did wake up, I was groggy for about an hour. Once I was fully awake, I felt OK. Not awful, but not exactly sunshine and roses.

Two days into the meds, I noticed a big change. My kids were staying with me, and my daughter barged into my room. It was Saturday, mid-morning. I was dead asleep. "Mommy, we spilled cereal!"

I hoisted myself out of bed and walked into the living room. There were my two kids, sitting on the floor and watching TV next to a lake of cereal and milk all over the carpet. "See Mommy!" my daughter pointed out. My soon looked up at me and immediately pointed at the culprit. "She did it!"

"Yes, I see it, and it doesn't matter who did it," I replied. "I guess we have to clean it up."

My response may not seem like a big deal, but it was. Before anti-depressants, I would have freaked out. There would have been yelling and anger and tears (from my kids, not me).

But with anti-depressants and all the work on self-awareness I had been doing in therapy, I was able to stop and think. "This is cereal and milk on the floor. It is not a big deal. It was an accident. It can easily be cleaned up. It is nothing to be angry about."

I was a new person. This was ... amazing. I looked the same on the outside, but I was completely different on the inside. The anxious, angry, impatient and judgmental person I had been was replaced with a more thoughtful, self-aware and even-tempered person. I loved the new me! Loved, loved, loved it! For the first time in months, I had something to be happy about.

Anti-depressants are not a cure-all, of course. I was still desperate for E. to stop seeing Stacy, but I was no longer a big, sobbing mess.

A week after I started the meds, E. and I talked in person. It was the discussion I had been waiting for. We talked about the future, the present and the kids. He gave me a big hug – and then he couldn't stop hugging me. "This feels so good!" he kept saying. We cuddled, and we made out. He had called things off with Stacy and was ready to start couples therapy.

Just like that, I was back in my beach chair, which was firmly planted in the sand.

It was May, and it was time to begin the hard work.

***

Rebuilding a marriage that had been savagely burned down to the ground sounds like a mission impossible. And yes, on the surface it is. Standing before a smoldering ruin is daunting. You have a huge mess to clean up before you even start to rebuild. Ugh. Who wants to deal with that? It's a lot of hard, dirty, exhausting, all-consuming work. Rebuilding is not for the faint of heart. You need to put your entire being into the process, and you need to take it slowly. Who wants to live in a house that was built in a week? Solid, high-quality buildings that are meant to last takes months – sometimes years – to complete.

As I learned, the best tools for this process are love and patience. Despite our sometimes dysfunctional dynamic, my old marriage had a solid, indestructible underpinning of love. We salvaged that foundation, filled in the gaps, and began building on top of it. This took time, but every step was worth it.

Once E. decided to give us a shot, we began spending a lot of time together while the kids were in school. The first thing we rebuilt was our sex life, which had never been great. Because I didn't feel wanted or attractive, I had a very low sex drive. I didn't feel sexy, I didn't feel connected to E. physically, and as a result, sex wasn't important to me. We could go three weeks without sex, and I wouldn't even notice.

E. would notice, though. Sex was always high on his priority list, so if our new marriage was going to work, sex needed to take center stage. It needed to be more frequent, more passionate, more fun and more adventurous. The new me was all in. At the ripe old age of 37, I knew that I was wanted. Being wanted and needed is intoxicating. It fueled my sex drive then, and it continues to do so now. So yeah, this party of rebuilding our marriage was awesome. (Sorry you had to read that Mom and Dad.)

Despite our passionate physical connection, E. held me at arm's length. He was not emotionally ready to let me back in all the way. I don't blame him one bit. After what I put him through, he was right to tread carefully and move forward slowly. Patience is not one of my virtues (as I have so amply demonstrated in this book), so I had to summon each bit of patience I could scavenge and just … sit and wait. I followed E.'s lead. Even when I wanted so badly to grab the reins and gallop forward, I stopped myself. I did a lot of self-talk that went something like: "Nope, not yet. Follow his lead. He is in charge. He is steering this process, not you."

It was good for both of us when I stepped back. Too often in the past, I had just charged forward like a bull. If I knocked something over, grazed someone or even ran someone down, I didn't care. I just kept going and ignored the mess in my wake. Now I thought through everything – my words, my actions and how they would impact me and those around me. I treaded lightly and tried my best to leave whatever was behind me in better shape than it had been.

Don't get me wrong. I was not suddenly subservient, timid or scared to be me. I was simply more mindful of my impact on people. Instead of criticizing or judging, I would ask, "Is this person or their actions impacting me? Does it matter? If I need to

94

respond, what is the best, most productive, most helpful response?" I know that seems very abstract, so here's an example.

E. is a grilling master. When he's at the helm, steaks come off the grill perfectly seasoned and caramelized on the outside and cooked medium-rare on the inside. But sometimes, the steak is not perfect. Maybe the fire is too hot, so the steak is a little burned on the ends and cooked medium. Does this warrant a stream of criticism? Nope. He did his best, he apologized it isn't as good as the last time, and we move on and enjoy our dinner. The old Monika would have criticized him through dinner and brought it up again the next time he grilled. Maybe I would have brought it up in front of friends. God, I cringe thinking about my old behavior. No wonder he had been so beaten down and had no energy to fight for me when Ryan came into the picture. But that's the truth about who I was – and why I am now so careful about my words and actions.

As E. and I spent time together, talking, cooking, running errands, etc. I intentionally demonstrated my new behaviors. He was keenly aware of these changes. It was hard not to see them! And then one day, E. said something that was so lovely and validating I nearly burst. "I miss you when we aren't together," he told me, "which is a very good sign!"

For the first time in a year, I was happy-ish. Not happy-happy, but happy enough.

An important part of our rebuilding process was therapy. It is beyond valuable to have the outside perspective of an expert. Our therapist, Marcia, was a PhD – she devoted years of study and training to become a family therapist. One of her specialties was couples counseling, and she proved to be an excellent guide. Of course, it takes more than a fabulous therapist to make it work. E. and I faced hard conversations head-on. We were very honest with each other and our therapist. We discussed what needed to change in our marriage and how to enact those changes (more on that later).

Even though we were making great progress, one thing was holding me back. I was distraught at the way I had treated E. I was ashamed of what I had done to our marriage. I was still angry with myself, and I admitted that I would not forgive myself until E. forgave me. I didn't assume he would forgive me. I hoped he would, but I couldn't tell him what to do. He had to work through his feelings and come to forgiveness on his own. This was a very heavy burden to bear, but I carried it with me. It was my penance. I deserved it, and I held onto it for as long as I needed to.

Now it was mid-June. We had been in couples counseling for a month. We began going on dates. We were making concrete, positive progress. Every day was filled with positivity and love, and every moment I spent with E. felt like a gift.

But there was one more big hurdle for me to leap over, and that hurdle was a person. It was Will. The first guy I had an affair with was still standing between E. and me. At one of our therapy sessions, E. brought him up. "In order for us to get back together, you need to admit to the affair with Will. I know you did it. You know you did it. But until you say out loud that you had an affair with him, we can't completely move forward. The lying about him has hampered our reconciliation."

Marcia and E. both looked at me, expectantly.

"Yes, I had an affair with Will," I said sheepishly.

"Thank you," E. responded. That was all he needed to hear.

Admitting to Will was another huge burden lifted off my shoulders, but I had one more thing to do. At E.'s request, I emailed Will.

Hi,

E. and I are getting back together and going through the painstaking process of rebuilding our marriage. In order for this to work, I am erasing you from my life. If I see you, I won't talk to you or even acknowledge you. If you email me, I won't respond. If you call me, I won't answer the phone or listen to your voicemail. And please do not respond to this email.

Thanks,
Monika

To Will's credit, he did not respond.

Much to my surprise, I have seen him only once since I sent that email; it was almost four years since E. and I got back together. I was in the middle of a meeting at a coffee shop, discussing a new project with a colleague. In my peripheral vision, I saw Will walk out of the restaurant next door. He saw me immediately and came over. He was literally standing next to me with a big sappy grin on his face. I couldn't ignore him, as much as I wanted to. Shit.

"Hi!" I said, as I got up.

"Hey Monika, it's great to see you," he said. And suddenly his arms were around me and he was squeezing me in one of his bear hugs and sighing. I knew that hug well. And I knew that sigh well. Too well. It was an I-want-you sigh.

I extricated myself from what was now an overly-long hug and introduced him to my friend.

"Will, this is Amy. We're working on a project together."

"Hi Will," she said.

"Hi Amy, great to meet you!" And then Will was nervously blubbering. "You are in fantastic hands with Monika. She is one of the best bloggers out there, so whatever she's doing for you will be perfect."

"Thanks Will, that's really sweet of you to say that." What else was I supposed to say? I just wanted the conversation to end.

"Well, I have to get back to work," he said. "Monika, it was great to see you as always. Amy, great to meet you."

"You too, Will!" she said. "Bye!"

I texted E. as soon as my meeting ended.

Don't freak out, but I just saw Will. I had to say hi because he interrupted a meeting. It was fine. It was weird.

E. texted right back: *OK, thanks for letting me know.*

And that was that.

***

One of the biggest surprises for me during couples counseling was how quickly E. said he trusted me. This admission came when we were talking about how I used to hide my phone from him. I would sneak around, making up excuses to meet with Will or work on nights and weekends so I could message with Ryan. I emailed with Will using a "secret" email address. I texted with Ryan almost nonstop. Now, I was making it a point to give E. access to my phone, computer and email. He was free to look at what I was up to online. He didn't want to, though.

"I trust you," he stated emphatically during one counseling session. "What I don't trust – and what scares me – is living through another disaster like last year. I can't do that again."

"Well, neither can I," I said.

Our therapist Marcia turned to him and said, "E., you need to pay attention and not passively trust Monika. Actively trust her. Pay attention, engage, ask questions and show your appreciation for each other. You don't need to read her texts or go through her email, but you can't take each other for granted."

Bingo.

Around this time, I started coming over to the house when the kids were there. We wanted them to see that we were getting along, but we were also planting the seeds of a new life as a happy family, all living under one roof with Mommy and Daddy back together. We treaded lightly around the kids, and I treaded lightly around the house, where I hadn't lived for months.

On Father's Day, E. and I prepared a big dinner to celebrate him. The kids were thrilled we were doing this together, and we had a great time, laughing and joking around like we always used to.

Later that night, E. and I were chatting on the phone. He confessed that my pitching in at the house made him anxious. He was quick to point out that I was not doing anything wrong. It was his problem, not mine. I was being collaborative and helpful, and I was not taking over. This was a relief for me to hear, and I was so glad he said something.

"Moving forward," he said, "I will pull you aside if something is bothering me, and we can discuss it privately."

"Yes, that would be great," I said. This was new for us. In the past, I would yell if something was bothering me. E. would just hold it in and not say anything. To discuss something immediately, calmly and in private, was a very healthy and much-needed change.

A few minutes after we got off the phone, I got a text from E.: *I love you.*

My heart melted.

***

The following week, our son finished kindergarten and our daughter finished third grade. My parents drove to Virginia to pick up the kids for a week at the beach so E. and I could attend to some very important business: moving my stuff back into our house. Even though packing and moving and unpacking generally sucks, this move did not suck. Quite the opposite. I'd never been so happy in my life. I joyfully packed boxes and bags and schlepped things home. During each drive from the apartment to the house, I'd glance back at my overloaded car to see the kids' clothes and toys, artwork, plants, tableware, food, files, blankets and sheets.

This move was also great exercise – my apartment was on the second floor of a three-story building. No elevators – only stairs! In the summer heat!

We left the furniture to our landscapers, who carefully loaded mattresses, dressers, couches and lamps into the back of their trailer. Over the past month, we had sold off a lot of old furniture in our house – much of it tainted with bad memories. The new start to our marriage was marked by new furniture and décor. It seemed fitting.

On July 18, I had my last session with my individual therapist. Our work together had come to a close. After months of handwringing, sobbing and hard questions, there was nothing left to talk about. Before I left, she said, "I am very proud of you, Monika. You have come a long way and changed a lot." I walked outside into the hot summer afternoon with a smile from ear to ear. I had changed. I had worked hard to change, and I had done it. I was a new Monika, and I loved this new Monika.

The rest of the summer was magnificent, mostly because it was so uneventful. The kids were beyond thrilled to have me back home. E. and I were both completely relaxed around each other. We settled into new routines and a kinder, gentler communication style.

Four months after my individual therapist dismissed me, our couples' therapist closed her book on us. Marcia declared, "You two have worked so hard, and now I think our work together is done."

***

E. and I built a new marriage that is better, stronger, more balanced and much happier than it ever was – or ever could have been. We are six years into this new marriage, and everything is still pretty darn awesome. Is it perfect? Of course not! There's no such thing as perfection in this messy dance called life. But we do strive to be great partners to each other, and that's all that counts.

100

So, what is our secret? How did our marriage overcome a mountain of trauma to become this shiny, gleaming ball of happy energy?

We both worked hard to cultivate self-awareness.

Self-awareness is a big buzzword in the personal development, self-help and executive leadership communities. It's an important concept that seems ridiculously simple. Too simple. Yet it can yield profound changes both personally and professionally.

Self-awareness is understanding why you behave the way you do. I worked on this for months in therapy, because I almost completely lacked self-awareness (remember, I was entitled and my behavior was rarely corrected – a dangerous combination). E. is naturally self-reflective and thoughtful, but he had to work on it as well.

One of the biggest breakthroughs for me was understanding why I had two affairs in a row and left E. in such a cruel, cold-hearted manner. For years, I was a stay-at-home mom, and I grew to hate it. It is an exhausting, thankless job. I didn't get paid, I didn't get thanked, and I was not valued (especially not by our society, which condemns mothers whether you work full-time or stay at home full-time). For six years, I was an invisible, forgotten member of society.

Then I started and grew a company. I was noticed! I was appreciated! I was paid! And I wanted more of this positive feedback. So, what did I do? I took an unhealthy, inappropriate break from my life as a wife and a mother to have fun.

I was also holding onto a lot of anger that had built up as a stay-at-home mom. This anger stemmed from fear – fear that my life was turning out very differently than I had imagined it would. I was scared things would never get better.

I began building up my self-awareness by second-guessing all decisions, big and small, that I made every day. Even if I was reaching for an apple to snack on, I took time to think about what I was doing and why. When E. and I were first back together, I would stop and think before I replied to a hard question. Sometimes, I wouldn't respond for a few minutes. E. wasn't used to this and would immediately ask, "Are you angry?"

"No, I'm not angry - just thinking," I'd respond.

The nice thing about cultivating self-awareness is that it becomes second-nature. I don't have to spend three minutes thinking about my response; I'll respond in a few seconds now.

I also raised my self-awareness by listing out the reasons I had an affair:

- I was not getting enough attention
- I was not being told I was appreciated
- I felt like I was taken for granted
- I felt invisible
- I never felt worthwhile
- I never felt good enough
- I had unrealistic expectations of myself and others

E. and I discussed this list at length, especially how to prevent these feelings from happening.

A third self-awareness exercise I did was list my good traits and bad traits – and E.'s good traits and bad traits. Whatever I thought of – no matter how ugly and awful it made me look – were listed.

I wrote this list out in April 2012.

Good traits:

- Fun and funny
- Smart
- Curious
- Do-er – happy to take the initiative
- Fantastic cook
- Adventurous and loves to travel

- Good conversationalist
- Helpful
- Loyal
- Protective
- Homebody – happier at home with family than out and about
- Energetic
- Good hostess
- Many interests – wine, food, the arts, gardening, snowboarding, etc.
- Big reader – like to learn new things
- Positive
- Thoughtful
- Motherly instincts
- Good planner
- Great writer

Bad traits (this is a pretty brutal list)
- Impatient
- Short temper
- Mean streak
- Quick to correct
- Cranky, especially without enough sleep
- Belittling at times
- Stubborn
- Slow to acknowledge when I'm wrong
- Impulsive – quick to act on things that need time to be evaluated; don't see the consequences of actions until the damage is done
- Lacking boundaries – curse and argue about adult things in front of the kids
- Unapologetic – sometimes lack the remorse and sincerity to be truly sorry
- Judgmental

Because this is not E.'s book, I'm not sharing the list of his qualities that I wrote up. Suffice it to say, this is an important exercise to do. Be honest with yourself.

You know the book The Five Love Languages by Gary Chapman, right? Have you ever read it? If you haven't, it's worth a read. The basic premise is that we like to receive love in one or two main ways. The way we show love to our spouse is typically the way WE like to receive it, not the way they like to. This can cause a lot of issues in a marriage, because you think you're always showing your spouse how much you love them, but they complain you rarely do! To fix this, you need to learn their language.

My main love language is words of affirmation. E.'s is physical touch. Once I learned that, it totally made sense. Now when we sit next to each other at a concert, I'll hold his hand. Or when we watch TV on the couch, I'll snuggle up with him. I am very aware of what he needs to feel loved, so I strive to "speak" his love language on a daily basis.

We love each other.

Can you believe that after all that we went through, we were able to resurrect all the love that had been thrown away? Well, I threw it away. E. had to let it go, reluctantly and while in a state of shock.

It never went anywhere, of course. You can't truly destroy love, because love is energy. You can turn your back on it. You can run from it. You can bury it. You can misplace it. When we were ready, we knew just where to find it. We picked it up, dusted it off and nurtured it back to health. Because we had built up so much love over the years, this was a quick process.

You need that love! A relationship is nothing if it doesn't have a genuine and abundant amount of love around it. E. and I were absolutely committed to reclaiming and rebuilding that love. Luckily, I still loved much of what made E. "E." And I really loved the new aspects of himself that he worked on to improve our relationship and marriage.

He still loved my "old" good qualities, listed above. He also loved my "new" good qualities that I had worked so hard one. I still have some of my old bad qualities, of course. I'm not perfect! I am cranky without enough sleep. I can be stubborn. I am still impatient and impulsive sometimes. But I'm much more aware of these qualities. I know they're there, I recognize them when they pop up, and I try to stop and think if this quality or emotion is helpful for me right now.

A lot of those bad qualities, though? They are mostly – if not completely – gone. The mean streak, belittling, judging, slow admission that I am wrong ... they are not welcome in my heart or my life. Once I learned how much poison those qualities were bringing to my marriage, I worked hard to ban them.

We respect each other.

In the past, our arguments and disagreements often escalated into ugly behavior – my ugly behavior. I would completely dismiss E.'s viewpoint or idea. I didn't listen to him. I didn't consider his thoughts or feelings. He was just outright wrong, and that was that. Talk about ugly.

Somewhere in our relationship, I had lost respect for E. I didn't respect him as a person, and I didn't respect what he had to say. All that mattered was me. Of course, I'd give in sometimes, and then I'd act like a petulant baby.

You did not have to agree with someone. You don't have to love rock-climbing, attending the ballet, rehabbing old Mustangs or playing soccer every Tuesday night in a pick-up league. But you have to respect those differences. You have to respect that this is what your spouse loves to do. Those differences are not just OK, they're important. Imagine if we were all the same – how boring would life be? It is our differences that make life and relationships interesting.

As a side note, it's very important for you and your spouse to have different interests. You might join them on occasion, or you might pursue your own interests or hobbies. That's awesome, and it's healthy.

We appreciate each other.

As you know very well by now, I was very dismissive of E. in our "old marriage." The qualities that I first loved about him – his easy-going character, his ability to connect with and have a fantastic conversation with anyone, his analytical mind, his deliberate decision-making – were overshadowed by my own unhappiness. I began taking him for granted, and I stopped admiring him.

Because of how badly Ryan had treated me, I was slowly able to see how precious E.'s good qualities are. Not everyone has those qualities! And some of them are super rare! Once I listed out his good qualities, my appreciation (and respect) for E. increased exponentially. I really thought about who he is and why his traits are so important to me. I took time to understand how he thinks and how deep his feelings run.

I am a very quick decision-maker – verging on impulsive. E. deliberates and carefully thinks through pros and cons before he reaches a decision. This comes in handy when making big decisions, like, oh, buying a house or a car. In fact, I don't go car shopping. E. does. E. comes home in the car make and model we agreed upon. I would come home in the most expensive model, all tricked out with every bell and whistle, simply because it drives so well and the sale person was so nice and I really liked it so I got it.

Yes, his deliberate-ness annoys me sometimes. But instead of stewing about it, I tell him I'm annoyed. We talk about what he's thinking or where he is in his research. We have a calm, rational discussion.

It's much better than, "You spent *what* on that car?"

We are completely honest with each other.

Lying – whether it's hiding the truth or outright deception – has no place in a marriage. A marriage cannot survive and thrive without complete honesty by both partners.

Would things have turned out differently had I been honest about how invisible I felt or how unhappy I was? What if I had come clean about the first affair and asked for help? What if E. had told me that my behavior was destroying him and causing him to detach from our marriage? What if he had said, "We are going to marriage counseling, because your sense of entitlement is out of control"? What if we had set aside time to talk about our marriage and our goals instead of just living parallel lives?

Until I began the first affair, I don't remember ever lying to E. But our marriage was littered with conversations that never happened. We were hiding the truth about who we were and what we were feeling, and that was just as destructive. Instead of one big bomb going off, it was a lot of chipping away. Eventually, you get the same result: a destroyed marriage.

Being honest may cause a little or a lot of hurt. Your spouse may be surprised, or they may be angry (or both!). It may cause you to have a three-hour heart-to-heart talk. It may result in someone sleeping on the couch for a couple of nights.

The sooner you are honest about what's really going on in your life or your head, the better it is for everyone involved.

We trust each other.

An affair is like a Category 5 hurricane when it comes to trust in a marriage. It's gone in an instant – and it can take months or years to rebuild.

You can try to regain trust with words alone, but actions are much more important. Not action – actions. Plural. You need to consistently behave in a way that rebuilds trust.

One of the ways I regained E.'s trust was with a list (yes, I love lists). I began a daily list of how my actions had changed, both due to my increased self-awareness and the meds. That way, E. could understand how I had changed even when we weren't together. This was important, because when we first began rebuilding our marriage, we were not living together. I was living in the apartment, and E. was living in our house. Because I had initiated this reconciliation and tearfully begged E. so many times on the phone to please take me back, he trusted that I would do whatever it took. He didn't necessarily trust me, but he trusted my intentions.

Every day, I created a list of my actions and sent it to him. When we were together, he could see my actions first-hand. I focused on being the "new" Monika and demonstrating that I was, indeed, different and better. His trust in me began to build, until one day, there it was, a glowing neon sign in the pitch black.

I became much more selfless.

One of my favorite parts of Christmas is watching my family open their gifts. I love to see their surprise and happiness to the point that I don't even care if I open my gifts. Their happiness becomes my happiness.

Well, now I'm like that on more than one day out of the whole damn year. After causing so much misery for so many people for so long, all I want to do is make other people happy. This is not to say I turned into a doormat – egads, no! My family and friends will laugh when they read that. Instead, I try to think about things from other people's viewpoint much more often. What would they like? What will make them (not just me) happy?

We talk.

When I talked about honesty, I alluded to how important it is to talk to your spouse. Think of it like checking in with your team at work. Ask how things are going. Ask what you can do better or change. Ask if there's anything they want to discuss. Don't assume that your spouse will bring something up. Be engaged with them, and ask!

E. and I used to check in on a regular basis. Once we got back into a nice groove with our marriage, our check ins became more random. But we do check in! We are very aware of when the other person is out of sorts – for whatever reason – so when we notice something amiss, we ask, "Is everything all right?"

Don't think that you can every stop talking. You need to keep those lines of communication open. What would happen at work if you never told one of your subordinates that you weren't happy with their performance? Eventually, you'd be so angry about constantly having to fix their messes that you'd resent them. Things would escalate or implode from there, affecting your team, your department and even the entire company.

Even with all the work I've done, it can still be hard to bring up an issue that's bothering me. Sometimes I don't know where to start. Sometimes it may take a few days to find a quiet time to chat (if you're a parent, you know how hard that can be!). But don't let one week slide by, and then another and another. Soon six months have flown by, and you have no idea how the other person is doing, what they're feeling, what they've been thinking about, etc. Meanwhile, the resentment might be building – and they have no idea it's even happening.

We prioritize each other.

I tell E. all the time that he's my favorite human. I prioritize spending time with him over our kids (yes, I said it), hanging with friends, and especially working. I love our kids to bits. I love spending time with (and having long conversations with) my friends. I love the satisfaction of working and helping clients reach their goals. But none of those people and activities are more important than my husband.

When E. talks to me, I look him in the eye or at least acknowledge that I'm actively listening. I laugh at his jokes. I ask for his input. I share good news with him first. I call him when I'm upset and need to talk. And vice versa. We have each other's backs, and I consider it an honor and a privilege to be in love with my best friend.

Spending quality one-on-one time with your spouse WITHOUT distractions is one of the best things you can do for your marriage. Snuggling on the couch while you binge-watch Game of Thrones is all well and good, but that's not quality time. You're not interacting. You're not connecting. You're not completely tuned into each other. You're simply tuned into HBO and sharing space on the couch.

Maybe you need to set up regular (weekly or biweekly) date nights. Maybe you need to set aside one night a week, after the kids are in bed, to kick back with a bottle of wine and just ... talk. Maybe once every six months you can escape for a long weekend. No kids, no dogs, no friends, no family. Just the two of you. What you do doesn't matter as long as you are committed to prioritizing time with your spouse over other obligations.

Our kids are in middle and high school now. They're older and more independent, so it's easier for E. and me to spend time together ... alone. Yes, sometimes we can be lazy about it. Sometimes life gets in the way (I'm looking at you, start-of-school-year and end-of-school-year). Sometimes one of us is sick, or one of us is traveling for work. Life happens. Be mindful of these roadblocks, and figure out a solution together.

Prologue

As I write this, it's six plus years later. The painful memories of that wretched time in our lives have faded and been painted over by so many new wonderful memories.

Do I ever think about the affairs? About Will and Ryan? Sure, every once in a while. But when I do, there's no emotion there anymore. No love, regret, anger, guilt – nothing. Once I forgave myself, I let go of all negativity. It's the only way I could move forward. Plus, the affairs don't define me. They're part of my story, they aren't my story. They aren't me.

Friends still marvel at how strong, loving and outright happy our marriage is. "What you went through – and how you were able to save your marriage – it's so rare. We are so proud of you and so happy you were able to work it out. You're so lucky."

We are lucky. I'm grateful for who I am and what our marriage is. I am so grateful for E. and I thank my lucky stars that he's mine.

I do not wish my experience on anyone. Yes, I needed to make changes – some pretty big changes – both inside myself and inside my marriage. Recovering from a destructive affair was a painful, meandering to change. I don't recommend it. But I also don't judge if you're having an affair right now – or were having an affair and recently ended it – or are about to embark on one.

Here's one important thing I learned – it's one of the biggest lessons anyone can take from my experience: Think of your affair as a wake-up call. Use the experience as the shove you need to make changes. Examine your life and begin to create a happier, healthier, more fulfilling life, no matter what that might mean to you.

Stop and think about these questions: Who are you? What's important to you? What makes you happy? What is really going on with your marriage? Can your marriage be saved?

You might not have the answers, and that's OK. I can help you find the answers.

I created an online community called The Shelter for you. You need someone to talk to. Yes, individual therapy is great, but there's no substitution for talking to people who have been through (or are going through) a similar experience.

Think of The Shelter as group therapy. It is a loving, supportive community. You won't be judged. No one will point fingers at you. No one will make you feel ashamed. It's a completely safe space to be completely honest and candid. You can share your story, ask for insights and listen to objective advice from experts and other community members. You'll also get to talk to me.

I will admit that I'm really jealous you have this community, this space and this kind of support! I could have used it back in 2011 and 2012. As I wrote in the Introduction, a lot of my friends disappeared. They had no idea how to deal with me. The five people who didn't disappear could only offer so much support and encouragement. It was emotionally exhausting for me AND them. Talking to people who have been there, done that is powerful. It's support unlike any other you will receive. And again, it's a safe, judgment-free space.

But you'll get a lot more than a community eager to listen and help. You'll get access to a couple of programs that I'm really excited about. One will allow you to gain clarity around why you're having an affair and whether you can fix your marriage. Another will guide you as you transform your relationship with yourself. You'll get to connect with me and ask me questions. You'll be able to join Q&A sessions with experts in the fields of relationships, self-discovery and more. You'll be able to start taking the steps you need to chart a new course for your life.

Membership is open to men and women – gay, straight, bi, queer, trans – we don't discriminate! – who are thinking about having an affair, having one, trying to get out of one, or recently ended one. Members are strictly vetted, so please stop by and learn more:

https://www.theshelter.life/self-discovery-course/

You just read my story. You read about the heartbreak and devastation. Trust me that there is a way out. If I can build a healthier and happier marriage and life after two – not one, but two! – affairs, so can you.

I'll see you in The Shelter.

Acknowledgments

Next to rebuilding my marriage, writing this book was the hardest thing I've ever done. Without the encouragement of so many awesome people in my life, I could not have gotten this story published.

To Bob and MK, thank you for reading the first drafts and providing me with your feedback, insights and edits.

To Michelle, Hilary, Nicole, Mike and Tammy, thank you for your unwavering support and instilling me with the confidence that my story needed to be shared.

To all my friends who appeared in this book under various pseudonyms, I don't know what I did to deserve your friendship, but thank you for sticking by me during the darkest of my dark days.

To Mom, Dad and my brothers, thank you for believing in me when I didn't believe in myself.

To my kids, thank you for choosing me to be your mom. You inspire me to be a better person every single day.

E., you are my favorite. Thank you for everything.

About the Author

Monika Patton is a small business owner and first-time author. She lives with her husband, kids and dog in the 'burbs.

CPSIA information can be obtained
at www.ICGtesting.com
Printed in the USA
FFHW020702191219
57123226-62691FF